Deuteronomy 4
AND THE
Second Commandment

Studies in Biblical Literature

Hemchand Gossai
General Editor

Vol. 60

PETER LANG
New York • Washington, D.C./Baltimore • Bern
Frankfurt am Main • Berlin • Brussels • Vienna • Oxford

Knut Holter

Deuteronomy 4
AND THE
Second Commandment

PETER LANG
New York • Washington, D.C./Baltimore • Bern
Frankfurt am Main • Berlin • Brussels • Vienna • Oxford

Library of Congress Cataloging-in-Publication Data

Holter, Knut.
Deuteronomy 4 and the second commandment / Knut Holter.
p. cm. — (Studies in biblical literature; v. 60)
Includes bibliographical references and indexes.
1. Bible. O.T. Deuteronomy IV—Criticism, interpretation, etc.
2. Ten Commandments. I. Title: Deuteronomy four
and the second commandment. II. Title. III. Series.
BS1275.52.H65   222'.1506—dc21   2003011155
ISBN 0-8204-6823-1
ISSN 1089-0645

Bibliographic information published by **Die Deutsche Bibliothek**.
Die Deutsche Bibliothek lists this publication in the "Deutsche
Nationalbibliografie"; detailed bibliographic data is available
on the Internet at http://dnb.ddb.de/.

This book is published with support
from the Norwegian Research Council

The paper in this book meets the guidelines for permanence and durability
of the Committee on Production Guidelines for Book Longevity
of the Council of Library Resources.

Printed in Germany

To
the Old Testament Society of South Africa
in appreciation
for making me an honorary member

צפון וימין אתה בראתם

TABLE OF CONTENTS

EDITOR'S PREFACE

More than ever the horizons in biblical literature are being expanded beyond that which is immediately imagined; important new methodological, theological, and hermeneutical directions are being explored, often resulting in significant contributions to the world of biblical scholarship. It is an exciting time for the academy as engagement in biblical studies continues to be heightened.

This series seeks to make available to scholars and institutions, scholarship of a high order, and which will make a significant contribution to the ongoing biblical discourse. This series includes established and innovative directions, covering general and particular areas in biblical study. For every volume considered for this series, we explore the question as to whether the study will push the horizons of biblical scholarship. The answer must be *yes* for inclusion.

In this volume Knut Holter explores the interpretive accents of Deuteronomy 4, of the Second commandment. Holter argues cogently and persuasively that the interpreter of Deuteronomy 4 is seeking to relate the commandment to the particular concerns and context in which the interpreter finds himself. Beyond the technical and scrupulous examination of the text lies a critical issue, and that is the manner in which one interprets a text in light of ever-changing circumstances, while maintaining the integrity of the text. The horizon has been expanded.

Hemchand Gossai, Series Editor

ACKNOWLEDGMENTS

Most of the research for this book was made during a sabbatical back in 2000. My sincere thanks go to the School of Mission and Theology (Stavanger) for granting me a break from the burden and heat of the day; to the Non-Fiction Literature Fund (Oslo) for a travel grant enabling me to spend some time in Rome; and to the Biblicum Library (Rome) for allowing me into its treasury. Also, I am grateful to Prof Kirsten Nielsen (University of Aarhus), Prof Hendrik Bosman (University of Stellenbosch), and Prof Magnar Kartveit (School of Mission and Theology, Stavanger), who read the manuscript and encouraged me to have it published. Finally, I would like to thank Prof Hemchand Gossai (Muhlenberg College, Allentown) for accepting the manuscript for publication in the *Studies in Biblical Literature* series, and the Norwegian Research Council (Oslo) for a grant that covers the printing subsidies.

Stavanger, July 2003

Knut Holter

• CHAPTER ONE •

INTRODUCTION

You shall not make for yourself a graven image, says the Second commandment (Deut 5:8, Exod 20:3)—thereby pinpointing the Old Testament ban on images, a ban which not only was of great importance to the ancient Israelites, according to the Old Testament, but which also has played an important role amongst their heirs within the post-biblical traditions of Judaism, Christianity and Islam.

In its dignified and clear-cut Decalogue version, the commandment rises above all what's, why's, and how's, and throughout more than two millennia its interpreters have struggled with its ban on images. On the one hand, Jewish, Christian and Islamic theologians have explored the theological meaning and practical implications of the commandment. Attempting to express verbally its depths and breadths, they have built it into different kinds of broader theological systems. But then, on the other hand, artists within the same religious traditions have also given the commandment their interpretations. More or less dependent on the verbal expressions of the theologians they have struggled with the difficult task of visualizing the Decalogue's ban on images.

However, theologians and artists within the post-biblical traditions of Judaism, Christianity and Islam were not the first ones to struggle with the theological meaning and practical implications of this commandment. Further back in its history of interpretation the Second commandment seems to have represented a problem and a challenge to theologians and artists in Old Testament times as well. The work of the performers of the visual arts and how it came to grips with the commandment will be omitted here. The present investigation will instead focus on what one could call the work of the performers of the textual arts, those theologians in Old Testament times whose texts represent attempts at relating the theological meaning and practical implications of the commandment to various broader sets of thoughts and acts. Examples of their textual work can be found throughout most of the Old Testament, and one of the most important ones is found in Deut 4.[1]

Deut 4 is an important example in this respect, not only because this single chapter offers the most comprehensive Old Testament accumulation of clear allusions to the Second commandment, but also because it offers a quite unique attempt, at least as far as the Old Testament is concerned, at giving the commandment a theological rationale:

> *Watch yourselves carefully, since you did not see any form* (כל־תמונה)
> *on the day that Yahweh spoke to you at Horeb out of the midst of the*
> *fire; beware so that you do not become corrupt and make for*
> *yourselves an image, the form of any* (תמונת כל־) *figure,* [...] (vv. 15–
> 16a).

One would expect that Deut 4's comprehensive accumulation of clear allusions to the Second commandment, combined with its unique attempt at giving the commandment a theological rationale, would make this chapter a central source in the current exegetical and religio-historical discussion about the ban on images in ancient Israel's religion. This, however, is hardly the case. On the one hand, scholars who approach this discussion from exegetical perspectives, tend to emphasize literary critical questions related to genetic models for a supposedly

---

[1]   With the expression "Deut 4" is here and throughout the present investigation meant its vv. 1–40. Irrespective of the questions of the textual genesis and literary organizing of vv. 1–40 (cf. below, pp. 6–13), it is generally acknowledged that these verses form a unit that is distinct from its textual context: the preceding instructions to the Transjordanian tribes (Deut 3:18–22) and prayer of Moses (Deut 3:23–29), and the following assignment by Moses of the cities of refuge in Transjordan (Deut 4:41–43) and the introduction to the exposition of the law in chs. 5–26 (Deut 4:44–49).

textual growth of Deut 4, often with a quite atomizing result.[2] On the other hand, scholars who approach this discussion from more typically religio-historical perspectives, tend to simply paraphrase the text, or, at best, echo the genetic models of the exegetes and then build them into broader models for understanding the development of the religion of ancient Israel.[3] Common to both approaches is therefore, unfortunately, a lack of sensitivity for the overall structure, and thereby obviously also the overall message of this important chapter.

Some preliminary observations in Deut 4

A superficial reading through of Deut 4 is enough to realize the particular interest of this chapter for the Second commandment of the Decalogue (Deut 5:8–10, Exod 20:3–5): in this single chapter the opening line of the commandment (abbreviated "C")—"You shall not make for yourself an image, any likeness of [...]"—is alluded to (abbreviated "A") not less than three times:

[...]	תמונה	כל־	פסל	לך	תעשה	לא־	C 5:8
כל־	תמונת		פסל	לכם	ועשיתם		A 4:16
כל	תמונת		פסל	לכם	ועשיתם		A 4:23
כל	תמונת		פסל		ועשיתם		A 4:25

These three allusions to the opening line of the Second commandment are probably the clearest examples of the correspondence between Deut 4 and the commandment, but they are by no means the only ones. Scattered throughout the whole chapter, and in particular

---

[2]   Two major contributions here are C. Dohmen, *Das Bilderverbot* (1987), cf. especially pp. 200–210; and D. Knapp, *Deuteronomium 4* (1987) *passim*. Other recent examples include B.B. Schmidt, "The aniconic tradition", D.V. Edelman (ed.), *The Triumph of Elohim* (1995) 75–105; and T.N.D. Mettinger, "Israelite aniconism: developments and origins", K. Van der Toorn (ed.), *The Image and the Book* (1997) 173–204.

[3]   Amongst the many recent contributions, cf. S. Schroer, *In Israel gab es Bilder* (1987) 161–163; O. Keel & C. Uehlinger, *Göttinnen, Götter und Gottessymbole* (1992) 344, 363, 396; T.N.D. Mettinger, *No Graven Image?* (1995), 15, 25; and A. Berlejung, *Die Theologie der Bilder* (1998) 348.

concentrated around these three obvious allusions, are a number of others examples.

The correspondence between Deut 4 and the Second commandment has of course been acknowledged by critical interpreters for a long time. Some have noticed one or two sporadic examples of allusions to the commandment in Deut 4. Others have noticed more examples, arguing that the number of allusions is so high that it makes the Second commandment the major topic of the chapter. And others again have argued that some of the allusions reflect a correspondence between the two texts that is so strong that it can only be explained as a result of being touched by the same hand.

However, there is one element in the various examples of correspondences between Deut 4 and the Second commandment which is generally neglected by critical interpreters, namely the fact that the terminological and structural organisation of these examples of allusions successively follows the order of the commandment itself. I find this to be a very striking characteristic of the chapter: its interpretation of the Second commandment not only comments on certain important and/or accidental parts of the commandment, it actually comments on the commandment as a whole, part by part. A brief attempt at outlining this structure follows.

The first allusion is linked to the first example of what I just presented as three allusions of the opening line of the commandment: v. 16a alludes to Deut 5:8aα. But v. 16 is also prepared in the preceding verses: the key expression פסל כל־תמונה of the commandment is gradually pointed out from v. 12 on; v. 12 introduces the noun תמונה, then v. 15 repeats it and links it to a כל, thereby getting the accurate commandment expression כל־תמונה, and then finally v. 16 adds the noun פסל, similar to the commandment, but inverts כל־תמונה to תמונת כל־:

	תמונה	כל־	פסל	לך	תעשה	לא־	C	5:8aα
	תמונה						A	4:12
	תמונה	כל־					A	4:15
כל־	תמונת		פסל	לכם	ועשיתם		A	4:16a

The second allusion to the commandment is found in vv. 17–18, and it functions as an interpretation of the rest of the commandment in Deut 5:8: the 3x אשר-sentences here allude to the corresponding 3x אשר-sentences in Deut 5:8aβ–b, although the two first have changed order:

אשר בשמים ממעל ואשר בארץ מתחת ואשר במים מתחת לארץ	C	5:8aβ–b
אשר בארץ אשר ... בשמים אשר במים מתחת לארץ	A	4:17–18

The third allusion to the commandment is found in v. 19. The commandment has now left v. 8, and v. 9 is opened by the verb pair חוה and עבד, with the personal pronouns להם and ם- as objects. V. 19 follows this up with the same verb pair and the same personal pronouns:

לא־ תשתחוה להם ולא תעבדם	C	5:9a
ופן־ ... והשתחוית להם ועבתדם	A	4:19

The fourth allusion to the commandment is found in vv. 23–24. Here, v. 23b repeats the opening line of the commandment (5:8aα), perhaps in order to emphasize the context; this functions as an introduction to v. 24, which alludes to the motivation of the commandment, כי אנכי יהוה אלהיך אל קנא (5:9bα):

לא תעשה לך פסל כל־תמונה כי אנכי יהוה אל קנא	C	5:8aα.9bα
ועשיתם לכם פסל תמונת כל כי יהוה אל קנא	A	4:23b–24

Finally, the fifth allusion to the commandment is found in v. 25. Again, the opening line of the commandment (5:8aα) is repeated, this time as a conclusion to the other reference, rather than as an introduction, as is the case in vv. 23–24. And the phrase that thereby is pointed out is v. 25aα's בנים ובני בנים, which alludes to the בנים of the commandment (5:9bβ). At this place, however, only one single word, בנים, is alluded to, but this word is then developed into the expression בנים ובני בנים. There seems to have been a change in strategy here: the first half of the commandment (Deut 5:8–9a) has been alluded to more or less *verbatim*, whereas the second half of the commandment (Deut 5:9b–10), with its illustration of the punishment (exile) and love (repentence) that Israel eventually will experience in the future, is alluded to only by one single key word, the בנים that represent this future:

לא־ תעשה־לך פסל כל־תמונה על־בנים	C	5:8aα+9bβ
בנים ובני בנים	A	4:25aα
ועשיתם פסל תמונת כל	A	4:25bα

Summing up so far, I have attempted to demonstrate (i) that Deut 4 contains a number of allusions to the Second commandment, and (ii) that the terminological and structural organizing of these allusions successively follows the order of the commandment itself. Against this background I will argue that central parts of Deut 4 is made up of some sort of a word-by-word or phrase-by-phrase successive interpretation of the commandment. This successive interpretation of the Second commandment, and its function within Deut 4, is the object of the present investigation.

However, this is an object which immediately raises several more principal questions. These can roughly be grouped in two. First, questions related to the context of this successive interpretation of the Second commandment; how does Deut 4's interpretation of the commandment relate more generally to the questions of the textual genesis and literary organizing of the chapter? Secondly, questions related to a methodology for approaching this successive interpretation of the Second commandment; how are we to interpret a text that itself is an interpretation of a text, and in this case even a text to which we have access? Before we proceed to a closer analysis of Deut 4 (chs. 2–8), these two sets of questions need some further attention.

Context: Textual genesis and literary organizing of Deut 4

The questions of textual genesis and literary organizing are closely interrelated in the research history of Deuteronomy.[4] From the breakthrough of modern Deuteronomy research in the 19th century—represented for example by the early 19th century relating of a so-called early version of Deuteronomy to the scroll found in the Jerusalem temple during the Josianic reforms (2 Kings 22–23),[5] and the late 19th century development of a literary critical criteriology for the tracing of the

---

[4]   For a research historical survey to Deuteronomy, cf. M.A. O'Brian, "The Book of Deuteronomy", *Currents in Research: Biblical Studies* 3 (1995) 95–128. The most detailed research history is still H.D. Preuss, *Deuteronomium* (1982). Some relevant analysis of the older contributions is also found in S. Loersch, *Das Deuteronomium und seine Deutungen* (1967).

[5]   This was the major achievment by W.M.L. de Wette, *Dissertatio critico exegetica qua Deuteronomium* (1805).

textual development of the book[6]—there has been a strong tendency of focusing on questions related to the textual genesis of the book, often at the cost of questions related to the literary organizing of the transmitted and final version of the book. This tendency, however, has to some extent been balanced by various foci of more recent Deuteronomy research, represented for example by the mid 20th century focus on Ancient Near Eastern parallels to the structure of the book as a whole,[7] and the late 20th century focus on stylistic and literary approaches.[8]

The tension between the questions of textual genesis and literary organizing of Deuteronomy as a whole is also reflected in the modern research history of Deut 4, where a tendency of focusing on questions related to its textual genesis has dominated.[9] The groundbreaking literary critical studies by W. Staerk and C. Steuernagel in the late 19th century saw various "hands" in Deut 4; they noticed various examples of logical, terminological and ideological inconsistencies, and they introduced the change of number as an important literary critical criterion.[10] Throughout the 20th century various sets of literary critical criteriology have been developed and refined, but they have still proved to be of a somewhat ambiguous character:[11] in recent years we have seen that the various sets of criteriology in the hands of some interpreters—such as for example S. Mittmann and D. Knapp—have been tools serving to advocate a many-

---

6   In addition to more general literary critical criteriology, the frequent change of number in the addressing of Israel (2.p.sg./2.p.pl.) was developed into a more particular criteriology for Deuteronomy by C. Steuernagel, *Der Rahmen des Deuteronomiums* (1894); and W. Staerk, *Das Deuteronomium* (1894).

7   See especially G.E. Mendenhall, *Law and Covenant in Israel and the Ancient Near East* (1955).

8   Early examples here are N. Lohfink, *Das Hauptgebot* (1963); and G. Braulik, *Die Mittel deuteronomischer Rhetorik* (1978).

9   For surveys of the discussion, see C. Begg, "The literary criticism of Deut 4:1–40", *Epheremides Theologicae Lovanienses* 56 (1980) 10–55; and D. Knapp, *Deuteronomium 4* (1987) 3–20.

10   See W. Staerk, *Das Deuteronomium* (1894) 79–80; and C. Steuernagel, *Der Rahmen des Deuteronomiums* (1894) 34–37.

11   For an analysis of various sets of criteriology applied to Deut 4, see K. Holter, "Literary critical studies of Deut 4", *Biblische Notizen* 81 (1996) 91–103.

layered interpretation of Deut 4,[12] whereas they in the hands of others—
such as for example G. Braulik and E. Otto—have been tools serving to
advocate a literary unity of the chapter.[13]

In parallel with a continuing focus on questions related to the
literary genesis of Deut 4, recent years have also seen that questions
related to the literary organizing of its transmitted and final version have
received increasing attention. A major figure here is G. Braulik, whose

---

[12]   S. Mittmann, *Deuteronomium 1,1–6,3 literarkritisch und traditionsgeschichtlich untersucht* (1975) 115–128, argues that Deut 1:1–6:3 is made
up of a *Grundschicht* that addresses Israel in 2.p.sg., and that then is
expanded by two narrative layers using 2.p.pl., then by three layers using
2.p.sg., and finally by some "nicht klassifizierbare Ergänzungen". Five of
these, that is all except the *Grundschicht*, are attested in Deut 4. Against
Mittmann, D. Knapp, *Deuteronomium 4* (1987), argues that the various
"hands" responsible for the textual growth in Deut 4 should not be
identified in shorter fragments, but rather in longer thematic units. The
change of number here maintains some of its criteriological significance,
but more emphasis is put on thematic and terminological variations. For
other examples of various versions of many-layered interpretations of Deut
4, see for example C.T. Begg, "The literary criticism of Deut 4,1–40",
Epheremides Theologicae Lovanienses 56 (1980) 10–55; E. Nielsen,
Deuteronomium (1995) 54–68; and T. Veijola, "Bundestheologische
Redaktion im Deuteronomium", T. Veijola (ed.), *Das Deuteronomium und
seine Querbeziehungen* (1996) 258–261.

[13]   G. Braulik has presented his literary critical analysis of Deut 4 in his
detailed and very critical recensions of Mittmann's and Knapp's
monographies: "Literarkritik und archäologische Stratigraphie"
[Mittmann], *Biblica* 59 (1978) 351–383, and "Literarkritik und die
Einrahmung von Gemälden" [Knapp], *Revue Biblique* 96 (1989) 266–286;
the research for the two thorough recensions reflects the unpublished part
of Braulik's 1973 Rome dissertation on Deut 4, see his *Die Mittel
deuteronomischer Rhetorik* (1978) viii. E. Otto, "Deuteronomium 4: Die
Pentateuchredaktion im Deuteronomiumsrahmen", T. Veijola (ed.), *Das
Deuteronomium und seine Querbeziehungen* (1996) 196–222, takes Deut 4
as a unity stemming from the Pentateuchal editor; cf. also his *Das
Deuteronomium im Pentateuch und Hexateuch* (2000) 167–175. For other
examples of interpretations advocating the literary unity of Deut 4 on
similar premises, see especially J.D. Levenson, "Who inserted the Book of
the Torah?", *Harvard Theological Review* 68 (1975) 203–233; and A.D.H.
Mayes, "Deuteronomy 4 and the literary critical criticism of
Deuteronomy", *Journal of Biblical Literature* 100 (1981) 24–30.

1978 monograph on Deut 4 emphasized stylistic and rhetorical concerns much stronger than what had been the case in previous works,[14] but some of the same concerns are also reflected in recent commentaries; one example is provided by C.J. Labuschagne,[15] another by D. Christensen,[16] and to some extent similar concerns are found in M. Weinfeld's commentary too.[17]

There are certainly aspects of this tension between the questions of textual genesis and literary organizing of Deuteronomy as a whole that are hardly possible to solve, as they reflect concerns of methodological approaches that to some extent are incompatible. One can not, for example, expect scholars interpreting the chapter from the principally diachronic perspective of traditional historical-critical approaches to agree on these issues with scholars interpreting it from the principally

---

[14] G. Braulik, *Die Mittel deuteronomischer Rhetorik* (1978); see also his *Deuteronomium 1–16,17* (1986) 38–47. Braulik builds on the approach developed by N. Lohfink in his investigation of Deut 5–11, *Das Hauptgebot* (1963), and Lohfink's more seminal application of the same principles on Deut 4 in his "Auslegung deuteronomischer Texte IV", *Bibel und Leben* 5 (1964) 247–256, republished in an expanded version as "Verkündigung des Hauptgebotes in der jüngsten Schicht des Deuteronomiums (Dt 4,1–40)" [1965], N. Lohfink, *Studien zum Deuteronomium und zur deuteronomischen Literatur I* (1990) 167–191.

[15] C.J. Labuschagne, *Deuteronomium IA* (1987) 223–296; a major emphasis in Labuschagne's commentary is the suggestion that the various segments of Deuteronomy are composed according to patterns employing symbolic numbers like 7, 11, 17, 26, and their multiples.

[16] D. Christensen, *Deuteronomium 1–11* (1991) 71–95; a major emphasis in Christensen's commentary is the suggestion that Deuteronomy is made up of five concentric units, as well as several similar structures within each unit. The analysis of each individual subunit is based on the conviction that Deuteronomy is not simply a prose composition, but is best explained as a didactic poem, composed to be recited publicly to music within a liturgical setting; for further discussion, see his "Prose and poetry in the Bible", *Zeitschrift für die alttestamentliche Wissenschaft* 97 (1985) 179–189, and "Form and structure in Deuteronomy 1–11", N. Lohfink (ed.), *Das Deuteronomium* (1985) 135–144.

[17] M. Weinfeld, *Deuteronomy 1–11* (1991) 193–230; in this commentary Weinfeld follows up the rhetorical concerns he had developed in his *Deuteronomy and the Deuteronomic School* (1972).

synchronic perspective of certain literary approaches. And vice versa.[18] Nevertheless, on a practical, text analytical level, the differences are not necessarily very large.

As for the present investigation, it reflects a principally diachronic approach to Deut 4 and to the Old Testament as a whole. In general, I would argue that the basic concerns of the traditional historical-critical approaches—and this includes traditional literary critical analysis—are relevant. When I, nevertheless, throughout this investigation interpret Deut 4 as a literary unity and also make use of insights gained from literary approaches, it reflects no preference for any ahistorical perspective. Rather, it reflects my conviction that Deut 4 simply justifies being approached as a literary unity. Negatively, I find that the various arguments used to advocate the existence of different "hands", "layers" or "blocks" are not convincing. And, positively, I find that the literary organizing of the chapter—its overall structure, and not least its successive interpretation of the Second commandment—seem to indicate that this chapter is best interpreted as a literary unity.[19]

As for the literary organizing of Deut 4,[20] there seems to be no major scholarly disagreement. In spite of approaching the chapter from diverse

---

[18]   Cf. for example the typically synchronic, literary analyses of Deut 4 by J.G. Millar, "Living at the place of decision", J.G. McConville & J.G. Millar, *Time and Place in Deuteronomy* (1994) 32–49; and S.A. Geller, "Fiery wisdom", *Sacred Enigmas* (1996) 30–61. In these articles the diachronic concerns of traditional historical-critical scholarship are mentioned, but not really discussed.

[19]   For details, see the subsequent analysis in chs. 2–8, where some of the various arguments will be discussed. However, I will not go into all details in the massive tradition of seeing different "hands", "layers", or blocks" in Deut 4. I will discuss it where it is of relevance to my main thesis, and as for the rest I generally concur with the advocacy for literary unity presented by G. Braulik in his two detailed, literary critical analyses "Literarkritik und archäologische Stratigraphie", *Biblica* 59 (1978) 351–383, and "Literarkritik und die Einrahmung von Gemälden", *Revue Biblique* 96 (1989) 266–286.

[20]   It can of course be questioned on what premises we ask for an "organizing" of the chapter; is there not a danger that we by our attempts at "organizing" it impose ideas and epistemological concepts that are very far from both text and original setting? S.A. Geller raises this issue in his very stimulating essay "Fiery wisdom", *Sacred Enigmas* (1996) 30–61. On the one hand Geller claims (p. 36) that Deut 4 on closer examination "[...] looks less like

methodological perspectives, scholars tend to agree about the major lines in its literary organizing,[21] although one, of course, should notice that this organizing is legitimized with just as methodologically diverse reasonings.[22]

---

a well-organized argument than a jumble of loosely linked themes", and he concludes (p. 38) that "We seem to have arrived at a working hypothesis of authorial incompetence." But then, on the other hand, he continues (p. 38): "Before we close the book on Deuteronomy 4, smugly complacent in our Hellenic enlightenment, it might be fair to oppose to this hypothesis of intellectual fecklessness one that assumes its author's competence as thinker." And that is the focus of the essay: an attempt at tracing the intellectual competence of the author of Deut 4, by describing the text's preference for thematic synthesis and paradox.

[21] Examples of interpreters seeing various "hands" in the chapter are D. Knapp, *Deuteronomium 4* (1987) 112–114, who finds three major units—each being enlarged by a later "hand": vv. 1–14 (vv. 1–4 + 9–14, enlarged by 5–8), 15–28 (vv. 15–16a* + 19–28, enlarged by 16b*–18), and 29–40 (vv. 29–35, enlarged by 36–49); and E. Nielsen, *Deuteronomium* (1995) 54–68, who finds three units—each reflecting various layers: vv. 1–8, 9–24, and 25–40. However, also interpreters advocating Deut 4 as a literary unity tend to see some of the same organizing. Both G. Braulik, *Die Mittel deuteronomischer Rhetorik* (1978) 13–76, and A.D.H. Mayes, "Deuteronomy 4 and the literary criticism of Deuteronomy", *Journal of Biblical Literature* 100 (1981) 23–52, 25, find six units: vv. 1–4, 5–8, 9–14, 15–22, 23–31, 32–40. C.L. Labuschagne, *Deuteronomium Deel I A* (1987) 227, advocates a similar organizing; however, here vv. 9–14 are split into vv. 9–10 and 11–14, and vv. 23–31 are split into vv. 23–24, 25–28, 29–31. A somewhat different organizing is advocated by D.L. Christensen, *Deuteronomy 1–11* (1991) 71–73, who, according to his prosodic analysis of the chapter, finds three units: vv. 1–10, 11–24, 25–40.

[22] Let me use the transition from v. 8 to v. 9 to exemplify this. On the one hand, the two verses have been argued to reflect two different hands. Traditional literary criticism, represented by S. Mittmann, *Deuteronomium 1,1–6,3* (1975) 118 (cf. also pp. 183–184), argues that a new unit (or better: layer) starts in v. 9, and Mittmann's main criterion is the change of the number of the addressee, from the plural of vv. 4–8 to the singular of vv. 9–10aα (to v. 10's אלהיך). More recent literary criticism, represented by D. Knapp, *Deuteronomium 4* (1987) 31–32, has lost some of the earlier confidence in the change of number as a literary critical criterion, and Knapp takes vv. 5–8 as an addition to vv. 1–4.9–14, arguing that v. 9 refers thematically as well as terminologically back to v. 4. On the other hand, the

Since the present investigation searches for Deut 4's successive interpretation of the Second commandment and the function of this interpretation within the chapter, I will let the literary organizing of the chapter be oriented towards the allusions to the Second commandment. From a terminological point of view we have seen above that the first term preparing for an interpretation of the commandment is the תמונה in v. 12, and that the last term is the בנים in v. 25. Each of these two terms are parts of logical structures that make up textual units or passages. The תמונה in v. 12 is part of a passage starting in v. 9 and stretching to v. 14: the logical structure of this passage is a focus on the verbal character of the Horeb theophany and its relationship to the transmission of Yahweh's "ten words".

Likewise, the בנים in v. 25 is part of a passage that starts in v. 25 and stretches to v. 31: the logical structure of this passage is a focus on the consequences of Israel's keeping or not keeping of the commandment against making images, and these consequences are described in terms of exile and repentence.

In between these two passages, there are two more. First, vv. 15–20: the logical structure here is a focus on an exemplification of the commandment against making images, and the passage relates the commandment to astral deities. And then vv. 21–24: the logical structure here is a focus on an exemplification of the consequences of provoking the anger of Yahweh by making images. Since most of the allusions to the Second commandment are consentrated to vv. 15–20, which means that much of the following analysis will be linked to these few verses, I will for practical reasons divide this passage in three: vv. 16b–18 stick out from its context due to its strict structure,[23] and the three (sub-)

---

two verses have been argued to reflect two different units too, written by the same hand. G. Braulik, *Die Mittel deuteronomischer Rhetorik* (1978) 29, who emphasizes stylistic and rhetorical perspectives, argues that a new unit starts in v. 9, but within the logical structure of the previous verses, and his criterion is thematic and syntactic changes. M. Weinfeld, *Deuteronomy 1–11* (1991) 221–223, he too emphasizing rhetorical perspectives, finds that a new unit starts in v. 9, and his criterion is terminological and thematic changes.

[23]   The structural and terminological pecularities of vv. 16b–18 are noticed by several interpreters. G. Braulik, *Die Mittel deuteronomischer Rhetoric* (1978) 42, takes them as examples of stylistic emphasis within the larger unit of vv. 15–22, whereas D. Knapp, *Deuteronomium 4* (1987) 88–91,

passages of vv. 15–20 will therefore be vv. 15–16a, vv. 16b–18, and vv. 19–20.

What then with the rest of vv. 1–40, that is vv. 1–8 and 32–40? We will later see that there are some connections between these two frame texts and the core text of the chapter, vv. 9–31, so that it is justified to take the frame texts as a prologue and epilogue, respectively. At the present stage I would just like to point out that the frame texts reflect signs of a concentric structure around the core text. One sign is the parallelism between vv. 7–8 and 33–34: both texts are made up by a series of rhetorical questions pointing out the uniqueness of Yahweh and Israel; vv. 5–8 let 2x מִי-questions point out the uniqueness of Israel's God, Yahweh, and Israel's just laws and rules, and vv. 33–34 let 2x הֲ-questions point out the uniqueness of Israel's experience with Yahweh. Another sign is the inclusio of vv. 1–2 and 40: both content (observance of the laws, Moses as mediator, the land given by Yahweh) and terminology (e.g. חֹק, אָנֹכִי, לְמַעַן, נָתַן) demonstrate the parallelism between the two. Against this background I will argue that a literary organizing of the chapter can look like this:

Prologue 1–8	Examples of concentricity:		
	1–2	Inclusio:	Decrees and laws
	7–8	Rhetorical questions:	2x מִי: what other people?
Core text 9–31	9–14	Elaborating 5:8aα	You saw no form
	15–16a	Elaborating 5:8aα	Form of any figure
	16b–18	Elaborating 5:8aβ-b	Likeness of male or female
	19–20	Elaborating 5:9a	Bow down and worship
	21–24	Elaborating 5:8aα+9a	Jealous God
	25–31	Elaborating 5:8aα+9b	Children and grandchildren
Epilogue 32–40	Examples of concentricity:		
	33–34	Rhetorical questions	2x הֲ: did a people?
	40	Inclusio:	Decrees and laws

takes them as a result of "another" hand than the one responsible for the neighbouring vv. 15–16a* and 19–28. Cf. below, ch. 4.

Method: A text that is an interpretation of another text

The fact that Old Testament texts in various ways reflect and refer to other Old Testament and Ancient Near Eastern motifs and texts has received increasing attention among biblical scholars in recent years. It should be admitted that—from a methodological point of view—these are difficult waters to navigate. It is so, partly because of the complexity of the issue itself, but partly also because biblical scholarship has not been able to agree on a clearly defined technical terminology. An illustrative example of the latter is the key term "intertextuality", a term that originally was introduced by the literary critic Julia Kristeva in the 1960s. Kristeva's term was eventually embraced by biblical scholars, and it has in the recent decade been developed into a key term in biblical scholarship.[24] Often, however, biblical scholars use the term in ways that deliberately differ from Kristeva's original concept.[25]

---

[24]   For a useful introduction to the main positions within this field of study, cf. P. Tull, "Intertextuality and the Hebrew Scriptures", *Currents in Research: Biblical Studies* 8 (2000) 59–90. From a research historical perspective, the growing role of the concept of intertextuality can be seen from how it has been focused in Old Testament conferences and essay collections throughout the 1990s. A recent example is the 16th congress of the International Organization for the Study of the Old Testament, Oslo 1998, which had a special panel on "Intertextuality and the Pluralism of Methods", cf. A. Lemaire & M. Sæbø (eds.), *Congress Volume Oslo 1998* (2000). Another example is the 10th joint meeting of the Society for Old Testament Study and Het Oudtestamentisch Werkgezelschaft in Nederland en België, Oxford 1997, which made intertextuality its major theme, cf. J.C. de Moor (ed.), *Intertextuality in Ugarit and Israel* (1998). Various sections in the Society of Biblical Literature also showed attention to the question of intertextuality quite early, cf. D.N. Fewell (ed.), *Reading Between Texts: Intertextuality and the Hebrew Bible* (1992). Of other examples, cf. Issue 69–70 of *Semeia*: G. Aichele & G.A. Philips (eds.), *Intertextuality and the Bible* (1995); and also C.A. Evans & S. Talmon (eds.), *The Quest for Context and Meaning* (1997).

[25]   Cf. e.g. K. Nielsen, "Intertextuality and Hebrew Bible", A. Lemaire & M. Sæbø (eds.), *Congress Volume Oslo 1998* (2000) 17–18: "What I present on the subject of intertextuality does *not* therefore correspond to Kristeva's definition, but it is nonetheless inspired *by* it." For a discussion, cf. B.D. Sommer, "Exegesis, allusion and intertextuality in the Hebrew Bible", *Vetus Testamentum* 56 (1996) 479–489.

I will argue that one—very roughly—should distinguish between two methodologically divergent approaches: a wider and a more narrow form of intertextuality. On the one hand there is a principally synchronic approach that analyzes the manifold connections between a certain text and the web of "texts" (in a wide meaning of the word) to which this text belongs: the perspective is here the (historical or contemporary) reader, and the focus is on the text itself. On the other hand there is a principally diachronic approach that analyzes the connection between a certain (Old Testament) source text and another (Old Testament) text alluding to this source text: the perspective is here the author, and the focus is on the alluding text's re-use of the source text.

From a chronological perspective, Deut 4 has traditionally been understood as younger than the Deut 5 Decalogue version of the Second commandment. This understanding of the chronological relationship between the two has been nuanced and challenged by some interpreters in recent times, as it has been suggested that some of the authors responsible for Deut 4 have also touched the final version of the Second commandment.[26] This suggestion will eventually be rejected in the present investigation, and the chronological relationship between the two texts will be taken as the commandment being the source text and Deut 4 a text alluding to this source text. Against this background I find the more narrow form of intertextuality—the diachronic and re-use-focused approach—to be the most relevant for the present investigation.

A major figure within this field of Old Testament interpretation is M. Fishbane. In a number of works, and in particular in his *Biblical Interpretation in Ancient Israel* (1985), Fishbane has meticulously explored what he calls "inner-biblical exegesis", that is the different ways in which various "older" Old Testament texts are re-used in other "younger" Old Testament texts.[27] Whereas previous scholarship mainly

---

[26] Cf. especially C. Dohmen, *Das Bilderverbot* (1985) 229.

[27] Cf. M. Fishbane, "Varia Deuteronomica", *Zeitschrift für die alttestamentliche Wissenschaft* 84 (1972) 349–352; *idem*, "Numbers 5:11–31: a study of law and scribal practice in Israel and the Ancient Near East", *Hebrew Union College Annual* 45 (1974) 25–43; *idem*, "The Qumran Pesher and traits of ancient hermeneutics", *Proceedings of the Sixth World Congress of Jewish Studies* 1 (1977) 97–114; *idem*, "On colophons, textual criticism and legal analogies", *Catholic Biblical Quarterly* 42 (1980) 438–449; *idem*, "Revelation and tradition: Aspects of inner-biblical exegesis", *Journal of Biblical Literature* 99 (1980) 343–361; *idem*, *Biblical*

had focused on the re-use of traditions and motifs, Fishbane turned the attention to the re-use of texts, and in his research he attempts to describe some of the complex dynamic between textual tradition (*traditum*) and transmission (*traditio*):

> The analytic effort is rewarded by insight into cultural processes of tradition and change in ancient Israel for which only the textual results survive. These processes bear on the scribal transmission of texts and the clarification of words; the adaption, harmonization and revaluation of legal rules; the theological re-use of laws or historical themes; and the explication or reapplication of prophecies for new times.[28]

Fishbane finds four main forms of inner-biblical exegesis: scribal comments and corrections, legal exegesis, aggadic exegesis, and mantological exegesis. To the present investigation the form he calls aggadic exegesis is of particular interest. The (re-)use of the term "aggadic" reflects Fishbane's conviction that the post-biblical, rabbinic aggadah had important inner-biblical precursors. Aggadic exegesis, he argues, ranges over all kinds of genres and texts in the Old Testament. Whereas, on the one hand, legal exegesis is concerned with a more narrow clarification or reinterpretation of a particular law, and, on the other hand, mantological exegesis is concerned with a reinterpretation for the future, aggadic exegesis has a wide and here-and-now profile, being concerned with "[...] how a particular law (or topos, or *theologoumenon*) can transcend its original focus, and become the basis of a new configuration of meaning."[29] Therefore, Fishbane argues, it is an important characteristic of aggadic exegesis that the genres of the *traditio* are often quite distinct from the genres of the inspiring

---

Interpretation in Ancient Israel (1985); *idem, The Garnments of Torah* (1989); *idem*, "Inner-biblical exegesis", M. Sæbø & al. (eds.), *Hebrew Bible / Old Testament I/1* (1996) 33–48; *idem*, "'Orally write therefore aurally right': An essay on Midrash", C.A. Evans & S. Talmon (eds.), *The Quest for Context and Meaning* (1997) 531–546; *idem*, "The Hebrew Bible and exegetical tradition", J.C. de Moor (ed.), *Intertextuality in Ugarit and Israel* (1998) 15–30; *idem*, "Types of biblical intertextuality", A. Lemaire & M. Sæbø (eds.), *Congress Volume Oslo 1998* (2000) 39–44.

[28]   M. Fishbane, "Inner-biblical exegesis", M. Sæbø & al. (eds.), *Hebrew Bible / Old Testament I/1* (1996) 35.

[29]   M. Fishbane, *Biblical Interpretation in Ancient Israel* (1985) 283.

traditum;[30] for example, laws and priestly rules are re-used in prophetic speeches or exhortations, and *theologoumena* are re-used in historical and prophetic narratives, as well as in psalms and sermons.[31] The distinctness with regard to genre can have various functions: in some cases the *traditio* may be used to transcend or replace the *traditum,* whereas in other cases the *traditum* is not cancelled by *traditio,* but rather supplemented.[32]

Fishbane's approach has of course been re-used and related to the subsequent methodological and hermeneutical debate by other scholars working within the same field of textual analysis.[33] Two recent monographs—written by two of Fishbane's students—may serve to exemplify the debate throughout the 1990s. One is B.D. Sommer, whose (1998) analysis of Isa 40–55's re-use of older texts provides a most relevant methodological discussion and terminological clarification.[34] The distinction between "exegesis" and "allusion" is here emphasized: the former aims at analyzing or explaining an older text, whereas the latter uses the older text for some new interpretive accent, for example as

---

[30]   Characteristically, Fishbane argues, traditions are first decontextualized from their received form, then aggadically reworked, and finally recontextualized in new literary ensembles. The first phase transform a *traditum* into a *traditio,* whereas in the second phase the new aggadic *traditio* becomes a *traditum* in its own right; cf. M. Fishbane, *Biblical Interpretation in Ancient Israel* (1985) 415.

[31]   M. Fishbane, *Biblical Interpretation in Ancient Israel* (1985) 414.

[32]   See M. Fishbane, *Biblical Interpretation in Ancient Israel* (1985) 408–440; see also his "Inner-biblical exegesis", M. Sæbø & al. (eds.), *Hebrew Bible / Old Testament* (1996) 43–44.

[33]   For an early response, cf. W. Roth (ed.), "Interpretation as scripture matrix: a panel on Fishbane's thesis", *Biblical Research* 35 (1990) 36–57. For further discussion, cf. L. Eslinger's critical analysis of Fishbane, "Inner-biblical exegesis and inner-biblical allusion: The question of category", *Vetus Testamentum* 42 (1992) 47–58; and B.D. Sommer's defense for Fishbane's approach, "Exegesis, allusion and intertextuality in the Hebrew Bible: A response to Lyle Eslinger", *Vetus Testamentum* 46 (1996) 479–489.

[34]   B.D. Sommer, *A Prophet Reads Scripture* (1998); for definitions, cf. pp. 6–31, and for Sommer's practical application, cf. *passim.*

a revision of or a polemic against the older text.[35] The stages through which the reader is moved to recognize the allusion are also described;[36] of special importance is here the function of the "marker" that identifies the evoked text, and thereby enables the reader to realize how the source text is used in the target text.[37] Concurring with Sommer's concerns, the following investigation will refer to Deut 4's re-use of the Second commandment as inner-biblical allusions rather than inner-biblical exegesis, and special attention will be paid to how the target texts use the allusions to the source texts to express new interpretive accents.

Another of Fishbane's students is B.M. Levinson, whose (1997) analysis of Deut 12–26's re-use of the Covenant Code (Exod 20:22–23:33) very strongly emphasizes the innovative aspect of Deuteronomy's re-use of older texts. In this case Fishbane's inner-biblical exegesis is challenged as being no longer able to "[...] provide a satisfactory model to describe the achievements of the authors of Deuteronomy. The

---

[35] B.D. Sommer, *A Prophet Reads Scripture* (1998) 17, criticizes Fishbane for using the term "exegesis" in a far too broad sense; it tends to be used about any case in which one Old Testament passage borrows from or is based on another. Sommer instead offers a more narrow definition: "By 'exegesis' I mean an attempt to analyze, explain, or give meaning to (or uncover meaning in) a text". Further, contrasting exegesis and allusion, he argues that "An exegetical text clarifies or transforms an earlier text; an allusive text utilizes an earlier text"; cf. also his "Exegesis, allusion and intertextuality in the Hebrew Bible", *Vetus Testamentum* 46 (1996) 479–489.

[36] Sommer's discussion of "allusion" builds on Z. Ben-Porrat, "The poetics of literary allusion", *PTL: A Journal for Descriptive Poetics and Theory of Literature* 1 (1976) 105–128, and Ben-Porat's four stages through which the reader is led to recognize the allusion and use elements from the source text to read the alluding text: (i) recognision of the marker; (ii) identification of the evoked text; (iii) modification of the interpretation of the sign in the alluding text; (iv) activation of the evoked text as a whole; cf. B.D. Sommer, *A Prophet Reads Scripture* (1998) 10–13.

[37] For a discussion of various forms and functions of markers, cf. B.D. Sommer, *A Prophet Reads Scripture* (1998) 11–12. More sceptical against such lists of markers is T. Stordalen, *Echoes of Eden* (2000) 58, who argues that they "[...] are often so intrinsic to European literary convention that they cannot be trusted in analysis of biblical literature." For a more general discussion, cf. H.F. Plett, "Intertextualities", H.F. Plett (ed.), *Intertextuality* (1991) 8–12.

concern of the authors of Deuteronomy was not to explicate older texts but to transform them".[38] Levinson's radical conclusions with regard to the relationship between Deut 12–26 and the Covenant Code cannot be directly transferred to Deut 4's re-use of the Second commandment. Still, his emphasizing of the innovative freedom by which older texts are being used for new interpretive accents is relevant for the present investigation.

Incidentally, one of Fishbane's first published studies concerns a central passage (and indeed a central observation) for the present investigation. In a brief note from 1972 he suggests that the list of creatures in Deut 4:16b–19a reverses the creation sequence of Gen 1:1–2:4a.[39] A decade later, in his *Biblical Interpretation in Ancient Israel* (1985), this preliminary observation is briefly related to his concept of aggadic exegesis, and as such it provides a most interesting illustration of the *traditum/traditio* phenomenon: two older texts—the Second commandment and Gen 1—are re-used and combined by Deut 4, and then, surprisingly, "[t]he result of this aggadic adaption, moreover, is to establish a distinct rhetorical nexus between the themes of creation and idolatry."[40]

I find Fishbane's remarks concerning Deut 4 very fascinating. Still, as they are parts of a broader survey that covers the Old Testament as a whole, they are for obvious reasons only of a suggestive and very brief nature. As such, however, they invite further and more detailed investigation of this chapter from a similar perspective, focusing on its allusions to the Second commandment. This is what I intend to do in the following, and the questions to be posed can then be summarized like this: What interpretive accents are reflected in Deut 4's successive allusions to the Second commandment?

---

[38] Cf. B.M. Levinson, *Deuteronomy and the Hermeneutics of Legal Innovation* (1997) 3–22, 15.

[39] M. Fishbane, "Varia Deuteronomica", *Zeitschrift für die alttestamentliche Wissenschaft* 84 (1972) 349; cf. also his "Torah and tradition", D.A. Knight (ed.), *Tradition and Theology in the Old Testament* (1977) 278–279.

[40] M. Fishbane, *Biblical Interpretation in Ancient Israel* (1985) 321–322, 322. The re-use of Gen 1:14–27 in Deut 4:16b–19a continues to play a role in Fishbane's analysis of inner-biblical exegesis; cf. most recently his "Types of biblical intertextuality", A. Lemaire & M. Sæbø (eds.), *Congress Volume Oslo 1998* (2000) 40–41. Unfortunately, however, Fishbane does not elaborate his understanding by going any deeper into the two texts.

• CHAPTER TWO •

YOU SAW NO FORM

ANALYSIS OF VV. 9-14

Let us start our search for Deut 4's interpretive accents vis-à-vis the Second commandment with an analysis of vv. 9–14, the first passage in the core (vv. 9–31) of the chapter.

> [9] *Be careful, and watch yourself closely so that you do not forget the things that your eyes saw, and so that they do not depart from your heart all the days of your life. And you shall make them known to your children and to your grandchildren;* [10] *the day that you stood before Yahweh your God at Horeb, then Yahweh said to me: "Assemble the people before me that I may let them hear my words so that they may learn to fear me all the days which they live in the land, and may teach their children."* [11] *You came near and stood at the foot of the mountain. And the mountain was burning with fire up to the heart of heavens; there was darkness, clouds, and thick mist.* [12] *Yahweh spoke to you out of midst of the fire. The sound of words you heard, but no form you saw; there was only a voice.* [13] *He declared to you his covenant, which he commanded you to do, the Decalogue, and he wrote them on two stone tablets.* [14] *And of me Yahweh commanded at that time that I should teach you the decrees and judgements, so that you can do them in the land that you are crossing into to occupy.*

Chapter 1 noticed one possible terminological marker in this passage, indicating an allusion to the Second commandment, that is the noun תמונה in v. 12's contrasting of the verbal and visual aspects of the Horeb theophany:

לא־תעשׂה לך פסל כל־ תמונה	C	5:8
ותמונה אינכם ראים	A	4:12

Against this background the passage will be analyzed from three perspectives: (1) the relationship between the verbal and visual aspects of the Horeb theophany, (2) the function of the noun תמונה, in the passage and in the chapter as a whole, and (3) the interpretive accent of the allusion.

The verbal and visual aspects of the Horeb theophany

The Horeb theophany plays an important role in the theology of Deuteronomy, and it is referred to—explicitly and implicitly—several times throughout the book. In the present passage the profiled centre of the reference to the Horeb theophany is found in v. 12a: "Yahweh spoke to you out of the midst of the fire". This profiled centre has a few close parallels elsewhere in Deuteronomy; one is found in the frame around the Decalogue in ch. 5 (vv. 2–5+22/23–33), and another is found in the narrative about the Golden Calf in ch. 9 (vv. 7–29).[41] The following examples should suffice to demonstrate the terminological correspondences between vv. 9–14 and the parallel passages in chs. 5 and 9:

---

[41] The name Horeb occurs in Deut 1:2.6.19, 4:10, 5:2, 9:8, 18:16 and 28:69 [ET 29:1] (cf. also the single reference to Sinai in 33:2), and the Horeb theophany is referred to in and around these references. In addition come some texts without any explicit reference to Horeb, but where the context and central phraseology indirectly refer to the Horeb theophany; cf. הר, "mountain" (4:11, 5:4.5.22.23, 9:9.9.10.15.15.21, 10:1.3.4.5.10), קל, "voice" (4:12.33.36, 5:22.23.24.25.26, 18:16), אשׁ, "fire" (4:11.12.15. 33.36, 5:4.5.22.23.24.25.26, 9:10.15, 10:4, 18:16) חשׁך, "darkness" (4:11, 5:23) ענן "clouds" (4:11, 5:22), ערפל, "thick darkness" (4:11, 5:22).

4:12	וידבר יהוה אליכם		מתוך האש
5:4	דבר יהוה עמכם	בהר	מתוך האש
5:22	דבר יהוה אל־כל־קהלכם	בהר	מתוך האש
9:10	דבר יהוה עמכם	בהר	מתוך האש

"Yahweh spoke to you": It is repeatedly emphasized in vv. 9–14 as well as in the parallel passages in chs. 5 and 9 that what Yahweh did at Horeb was to speak. However, this emphasis on the verbal aspect of the theophany is immediately balanced—in a more visual direction—when the sentence (also in its parallel versions) continues: "out of the midst of the fire". In other words, the focus on a verbal aspect of the Horeb theophany does not prevent the passages from emphasizing that the theophany had also a visual aspect; Yahweh's speaking to Israel was indeed accompanied by visual phenomena. The relationship between these two aspects of the theophany deserves further attention.

The verbal aspect of the theophany is expressed in various ways. First, it is expressed through a varied terminology. With regard to the grammatical predicates in the passages, Yahweh—the sender of the message—not only "speaks" (דבר, *piel*, v. 12, cp. 5:4.22.24.26.27.31, 9:10.28), but he also "says" (אמר, *qal*, v. 10, cf. 5:27, 9:25), "declares" (נגד, *hiph.*, v. 13, cf. 5:5), "commands" (צוה, *piel*, v. 13, cf. 4:14, 5:32.33, 9:12.16), and "lets hear" (שמע, *hiph.*, v. 10). These different expressions of "speaking" are balanced by Israel—the receiver of the message—who "listens" (שמע, *qal*, v. 12, cf. 5:23.24.25.26.27.27, 9:33) to Yahweh. At this point there are no major differences between vv. 9–14 and the two other Horeb passages. Secondly, the verbal aspect of the theophany is also reflected in the grammatical and logical objects of Yahweh's speech, although with a less varied terminology. V. 12 presents the logical object of Yahweh's speech with the word combination קול דברים ("sound of words"). These two words—קול ("sound", "voice", cf. 5:22.23.24.25.26, 9:23) and דברים ("words" [pl. and sg.], cf. 5:5.22, 9:10)—dominate the Horeb passages, although mainly one at a time. In vv. 9–14 there is one more occurrence of קול, at the end of v. 12, where it points back to the word combination קול דברים earlier in the verse: "there was only a voice". Further, there are three more occurrences of דברים. First in v. 9, where it refers to the Horeb experience as a whole:

the meaning here is "things" rather than "words" *per se.*[42] Then in v. 10, where it summarizes the verbal communication of the theophany: "I will let them hear my words". And finally, in v. 13, where this verbal communication is identified with the "ten words" or Decalogue.

Turning to the visual aspect of the Horeb theophany, we notice that the most frequent term to describe the visual phenomena accompanying Yahweh's speaking to Israel is אֵשׁ, "fire", partly found in the expression הָהָר בֹּעֵר בָּאֵשׁ, "the mountain burned with fire" (cf. 4:11, 5:23 and 9:15), and partly in the expression מִתּוֹךְ הָאֵשׁ, "out of the midst of the fire" (cf. 4:15.33.36, 5:4.22.24.26, 9:10, 10:4). A close parallel to the latter is found in 5:23, where Yahweh's voice instead is said to come מִתּוֹךְ הַחֹשֶׁךְ, "out of the darkness".[43] And different aspects of darkness are also central in the portrayal of Israel's visual experience at Horeb: חֹשֶׁךְ, "darkness" (cf. 4:11, 5:23), עֲרָפֶל, "thick darkness" (cf. 4:11, 5:22), and עָנָן, "clouds" (cf. 4:11, 5:22).

In v. 12 the verbal and visual aspects of the Horeb theophany are related to each other. First, as we have seen above, when v. 12a positively points out that: "Yahweh spoke to you out of the midst of the fire". Secondly, however, also negatively, when v. 12b points out that: "The sound of words you heard, but no form (תְּמוּנָה) you saw". There is, accordingly, a tension between the verbal and visual aspects of the theophany, and the noun תמונה is used to accentuate this tension. Before we go deeper into the relationship between these two aspects of the theophany here in vv. 9–14, some words should be said about two other examples in the same chapter, in which the same relationship is described.

The first example is v. 33, which relates the two in the form of a rhetorical question: "Has any people ever heard the voice of a god speaking out of the midst of the fire, as you have heard, and survived?" The question belongs to a series of rhetorical questions, vv. 32–34, and the function of this series is to make Israel realize the consequences of her experiences with Yahweh at Horeb. The Old Testament gives varied descriptions of theophanies. Still, when v. 33 expresses the idea that no

---

42   Cf. W.H. Schmidt, "דבר", *Theologisches Wörterbuch zum Alten Testament* 2 (1977) 112–113; still, this use of דבר clearly fits the concentration in this passage of the verbal aspect of the Horeb theophany.

43   The more frequently attested אֵשׁ is reflected in some Hebrew manuscripts (as a substitute or as an addition) and in the Septuagint rendering of this verse.

other people has ever heard a god speaking from the midst of a fire and still lived, one can hardly escape the impression that this is a deliberate reference to the Old Testament tradition that no man can "see God and live" (cf. Exod 33:20, Judg 6:22–24, Judg 13:19–23). V. 33, however, seems to substitute the visual aspect of encountering God in a theophany for a more specific verbal aspect. This idea is further elaborated in one of the other Horeb passages, Deut 5:24–27, where Moses, together with the tribe leaders and the elders of Israel are described as reflecting on their experiences at Horeb. V. 24a mentions both the visual and verbal aspects of the theophany: "Yahweh our God has shown us his glory[44] and his greatness, and we have heard his voice out of the midst of the fire." However, when the passage continues, the verbal aspect of the theophany gets all the attention and the visual aspect actually disappears. V. 24b lets Moses and the others conclude the verbal and visual reflection of v. 24a by focusing on the former only: "Today we have seen that a man can live even if God speaks with him." And v. 25 argues: "if we hear the voice of Yahweh our God any longer, we shall die". The fire is here in the service of the speech. Its purpose is to consume those who continue listening to the voice of Yahweh.

The second example is v. 36.[45] Even clearer than in v. 12, this verse presents the verbal and visual aspects of the theophany as parallels:

ליסרך	את־קלו השמיעך מן־השמים	v. 36a
ודבריו שמעת מתוך האש	את־אשו הגדולה הראך ועל־הארץ	v. 36b

From the beginning, lines a and b are clear parallels: vv. aα and bα are set up as structural and semantic parallels.[46] This includes the instruments of the theophany: Yahweh revealed himself to Israel, from heaven with "his

---

[44] The כבוד here provides a terminological link to the central Old Testament reference of the idea that no man can see God and live, see Exod 33:18.22.

[45] This verse is important from a tradition historical point of view, as it combines the ideas of Yahweh speaking "from heaven" and "from the midst of the fire". The two are presumably not seen as contradictory; cf. M. Weinfeld, *Deuteronomy 1–11* (1991) 212–213.

[46] The parallel structure of vv. 36 aα and bα: (i) preposition + def. art. + the word pair "heaven"/"earth"; (ii) the verbs "let hear"/"let see" in *hiph.* + suff. 2.p.sg.m.; (iii) *nota accusativi* + the word pair (with suff. 3.p.sg.m.) "voice"/"fire".

voice" and on earth with "his fire". But what about the end of the lines, are also vv. aβ and bβ parallels? Clearly, they are not structural and semantic parallels in the same way as vv. aα and bα. Still, it can hardly be denied that some parallel structures exist also here: both address Israel in 2.p.sg., and both refer to the concept of relıgous instruction: v. aβ directly ("to instruct you") and v. bβ indirectly ("his words you heard out of the midst of the fire"). Against this background I would say that the structure of v. 36 can be described as a parallel presentation of (i) the mode (vv. aα and bα) and (ii) the function (vv. aβ and bβ) of the verbal (v. a) and the visual (v. b) aspects of the Horeb theophany. On the one hand, the final sentence—"his words you heard out of the midst of the fire" (v. bβ)—is a parallel to v. aβ's "to instruct you". On the other hand, v. bβ concludes v. bα's focus on the visual aspect of the theophany. The very point of Yahweh letting Israel see his fire, accordingly, is not the fire *per se*, but rather that his words could be heard from the midst of this fire. Or, in other words: the function of the visual aspect of the theophany is to create a context for the verbal aspect.

Now, it is generally acknowledged that Deuteronomy emphasizes the verbal character of the Horeb theophany.[47] I would, however, argue that ch. 4 goes one step further. The two verses which have here been briefly examined, vv. 33 and 36, together with v. 12, seem to draw a picture of the Horeb theophany where the verbal aspect not only is emphasized at the cost of the visual aspect, but actually is seen as *the* theophany. In v. 12 two ways of experiencing a theophany—"hearing" and "seeing"—are presented, and the contrast between the two is expressed by the antithetic parallelism of v. 12b:[48]

אתם שמעים	קול דברים	v. 12bα
ראים	אינכם	ותמונה	v. 12bβ

The structurally parallel participles שמעים ("hearing") and ראים ("seeing") serve to contrast the two possible ways of experiencing a theophany, of which the latter is explicitly rejected (אינכם, "you did not"): Israel did hear, but she did not see. The verbal aspect of the theophany is then further emphasized through the structural contrasting

---

[47] For a survey, cf. I. Wilson, *Out of the Midst of the Fire* (1995) 89–97.

[48] To the parallelism in v. 12b, cf. G. Braulik, *Die Mittel deuteronomischer Rhetorik* (1978) 33–34.

of קול דברים and תמונה. And the result is utterly clear: what Israel did hear was "a sound of voices", and what it did not see was a "form". In other words, v. 12 expresses an understanding of the relationship between the verbal and visual aspects of the theophany in which the latter has no independent function; its function is simply to create a context for the real theophany, the verbal one.

This leads up to v. 13, where the implications of the theophany are described. This verse, like the two parallel Horeb passages, Deut 5:2–5+22/23–33 (vv. 2.3) and Deut 9:7–29 (vv. 9.11.15), uses of the term ברית ("covenant") to describe these implications. However, the three passages introduce the ברית in different ways. Deut 5 and 9 introduce it by the more frequent term כרת (*qal*, "cut", "make [a covenant]"): "Yahweh our God *made* a covenant with us at Horeb" (5:2, cf. also 5:3, 9:9), whereas ch. 4 uses the term נגד (*hiph.*, "declare") to introduce the ברית: "He *declared* to you his covenant" (v. 13). Let us take a closer look at the organizing of v. 13:

עשרת הדברים | ויגד לכם את בריתו אשר צוה אתכם לעשות	v. 13a
ויכתבם על שני לחות אבנים	v. 13b

Vv. 13a and 13b are linked together by their common initial *wyqtl* forms, ויגד, "he declared", and ויכתבם "he wrote them". The introductory ויגד in v. 13a conceptualizes Yahweh's covenant (בריתו) as something that can be communicated verbally.[49] Compared to the Horeb passages in chs. 5 and 9, it seems clear that the introductory נגד of v. 13aα reflects Deut 4's particular emphasizing of the verbal aspect of the Horeb experience. This is continued when v. 13aβ relates the covenant and the Decalogue, by the apposition עשרת הדברים. The introductory verb in v. 13b, ויכתבם ("he wrote them"), then has a double relationship: its initial position and *wyqtl* form links it to the initial verb ("he declared") in v. 13aα, whereas its plural suffix ("he wrote *them*") links it to the final apposition in v. 13aβ ("the ten words"). In other words, the verbally transmitted Horeb covenant is identified as the Decalogue.

---

49 Deut 5:5 lets נגד (*hiph.*) introduce דבר, but not ברית; see to this F. García-Lopez, "נגד", *Theologisches Wörterbuch zum Alten Testament* 5 (1986) 194. The word combination נגד (*hiph.*) and ברית is not found elsewhere in the Old Testament. However, it should be noticed that Hag 2:5 lets the verb כרת introduce דבר.

The function of the noun תמונה

There are ten occurrences of the noun תמונה in the Old Testament, and not less than half of these are found here in Deut 4. The ten occurrences can roughly be grouped in three.[50] First, three texts use the term תמונה in a visionary context, to denote a "form" or "shape" that is seen in an extraordinary way. The question of visibility is of importance in these texts; the underlying question is what it means to see a תמונה. Two of the texts use תמונה to describe how the form of Yahweh can be seen. Num 12:8 relates the expression תמונת יהוה, "the form of Yahweh", to a word field like "seeing" (נבט, *hiph.*) Yahweh, or even "speaking face to face (פה אל־פה) with him". Similarly, Ps 17:15 relates the expression תמונתך, "your [i.e. Yahweh's] form", to a word field like "I shall see your face (אחזה פניך) in righteousness". Also a third occurrence, Job 4:16, where תמונה is not referring to Yahweh but to some other "form", emphasizes the aspect of seeing the תמונה, and it relates this particular "form" to a word field like לנגד עיני, "in front of my eyes".[51] Secondly, five texts use the term תמונה in connection with the Second commandment. Two of these are the two versions of the commandment itself (Deut 5:8 and Exod 20:4), and the three remaining ones are those three clear allusions to the same commandment that will encounter us later in Deut 4, vv. 16, 23, and 25. The very point of all five texts is to forbid or to warn against any involvment in making an image in the "form" or "shape" of anything. And thirdly, there are the two texts here in our passage—ch.

---

[50]   The Old Testament use of the noun תמונה has in recent years been investigated by C. Dohmen and E.-J. Waschke; cf. C. Dohmen, *Das Bilderverbot* (1987) 219–223; and E.-J. Waschke, "תמונה", *Theologisches Wörterbuch zum Alten Testament* 8 (1995) 678–79. Previous scholarship tended to make a semantic division between תמונה as "Erscheinung" on the one hand, and as "durch Kunst geschaffene Figur" on the other hand, cf. e.g. W. Gesenius, *Hebräisches und aramäisches Handwörterbuch* (1962) 881. Dohmen and Waschke, however, argue that it is the same basic meaning of "form" or "shape" which is reflected in both groups. Dohmen and Waschke are both influenced by D. Knapp's literary critical analysis of Deut 4, which will be questioned below. Still, I find that their semantic analysis of the term is convincing.

[51]   Like Deut 4:12, also Job 4:16 combines the two terms קל and תמונה; here, however, without the contrastive function of Deut 4:12.

4's vv. 12 and 15—in which, as I will argue, a combination of the two former groups are found.

Let us take a closer look at the five occurrences of תמונה in Deut 4. As pointed out above, these five occurrences constitute not less than half of the ten Old Testament occurrences of תמונה, an accumulation that demonstrates its importance in this particular context:

you saw no form	תמונה	v. 12
you did not see any form	כל־ תמונה	v. 15
an image, the form of any ...	כל־ תמונת	v. 16
an image, the form of anything	כל תמונת	v. 23
an image, the form of anything	כל תמונת	v. 25

As pointed out above, the first occurrence, in v. 12, belongs to a context (vv. 9–14) where Israel is challenged to remember the Horeb theophany; Yahweh revealed himself through the "sound of words" (קל דברים) only, and not through any visible "form" (תמונה). The second occurrence of תמונה—the one in v. 15—echoes the one in v. 12; here, too, it is used to point out negatively (cf. לא ראיתם) the verbal character of the Horeb theophany. Syntactically the two verses form a chiasm,[52] and terminologically they are very close;[53] there is, actually, only one major terminological difference between the two, the development from תמונה in v. 12 to כל־תמונה in v. 15.

The third occurrence of תמונה in Deut 4, however, the one in v. 16, appears to have a function and meaning quite different from the two former ones. From a syntactic perspective, the כל־תמונה of v. 15 occurs invertedly as תמונת־כל in v. 16a,[54] and from a semantic perspective, the תמונה in v. 16a does not any longer refer to the Horeb theophany, but the

---

[52] In detail: vv. 12abα + 12bβ >< vv. 15bα + 15bβ.

[53] Of minor differences it should be noticed (i) that of the two semantically parallel sentences קול דברים אתם שמעים אליכם (v. 12a) and וידבר יהוה אליכם (v. 12bα), v. 15bβ echoes only the former, (ii) that the negated אינכם ראים of v. 12 is rendered לא ראיתם in v. 15, and (iii) that there is a change from *piel* imperf. of דבר in v. 12, to *piel* perf. in v. 15, and an adding of the two words ביום and בחרב, which, however, both are attested in v. 10, that is the textual context leading up to v. 12.

[54] The relationship between v. 15's כל־תמונה and v. 16's תמונת־כל will be discussed below, cf. pp. 40–46.

prohibition against the making of images: Israel is warned against making "for yourselves an image, the form of any (תמונת כל־) figure". This latter pattern of using the noun תמונה is then, with some modifications, continued also in its two last occurrences in Deut 4, the ones in vv. 23 and 25.

The five occurrences of תמונה throughout Deut 4, accordingly, have different functions and meanings, and the question is then how they relate to each other. According to D. Knapp, the תמונה-text in v. 12 and those two in vv. 15–16 belong to different text blocks, reflecting different hands in the textual growth of Deut 4. Knapp's literary critical analysis of Deut 4 leads him to argue that vv. 1–4+9–14 constitute the oldest block, a block challenging Israel to obey the words (cf. vv. 9.10.12) they heard at Horeb, i.e. the Decalogue (v. 13); vv. 5–8 are then supposed by Knapp to be a later addition. Vv. 15–16a*+19–28 then constitute the second block, chronologically speaking, a block focusing upon one particular of these ten words, i.e. the prohibition against images; vv. 16b*–18 are here supposed to be a later addition.[55] A similar division between vv. 14 and 15 had been suggested also previously, for example by M. Noth and G. von Rad.[56] But Knapp develops this suggestion, linking it particularly to the re-occurrence of v. 12's תמונה in vv. 15 ff. According to Knapp, the aspect of prohibition against making images is totally absent in the semantic function of the תמונה of the older block (vv. 1–4+9–14, v. 12); this aspect is developed by the hand responsible for the younger block (vv. 15–16a*+19–28). This later hand consciously used the term תמונה of the older block to link his particular message of prohibition against making images to the message of the already existing text, the description of the theophany. Knapp finds this to be a good example of how the Deuteronomistic *Fortschreibung* took place. Later hands within the Deuteronomistic movement proceeded from terminology in the already existing texts, and developed aspects that were not necessarily present in these texts.[57]

There are two basic problems with this interpretation. First, it presupposes that the introduction in vv. 15 ff. of a new theme necessarily

---

[55]   For a survey, cf. D. Knapp, *Deuteronomium 4* (1987) 112–114, 205–206.

[56]   M. Noth, *Überlieferungsgeschichtliche Studien* (1963) 38; G. von Rad, *Das fünfte Buch Mose* (1964) 36.

[57]   Cf. D. Knapp, *Deuteronomium 4* (1987) 68; cf. also C. Dohmen, *Das Bilderverbot* (1987) 218.

reflects the hand of a new author within the literary development of this chapter. G. von Rad is utterly clear when he comments upon the textual transition from the Horeb experience (vv. 9–14) to the prohibition against making images (vv. 15–20): "Das kann nicht ursprünglich sein".[58] And Knapp follows this up, first theoretically, as he develops a literary critical methodology where change of theme becomes a major criterion,[59] but then also practically, as his major criterion for dividing between the older block (vv. 1–4+9–14) and the younger one (vv. 15–16a*+19–28) is this introduction of a new theme.[60] This is hardly convincing. One thing is that we probably do injustice to the ancient authors, if we deny them the ability of dealing with more than one theme at a time. Why should they not be able to do so, when the final text expects the readers to be able to deal with a number of themes at a time? But of greater importance is that the supposed thematic difference between vv. 9–14, on the one hand, emphasizing the Horeb theophany and the declaration of the Decaogue (cf. עשׂרת הדברים, v. 13), and vv. 15 ff., on the other hand, focusing on one particular of the commandments of the very same Decalogue, is somewhat exaggerated. I would instead argue that we here have a text starting quite broadly with a reference to the Decalogue as a whole, and then focusing gradually more and more on one particular commandment, the Second commandment.[61]

Secondly, as is noticed also by G. Braulik,[62] Knapp's interpretation presupposes that it is likely that the noun תמונה actually is able to occur in v. 12 without any references to the Second commandment. Although Knapp admits that this first occurrence of תמונה represents a new accent within the first block (vv. 1–4+9–14), he nevertheless claims that it is the author of the second block (vv. 15–16a*+19–28) who is the first to relate

---

[58]   G. von Rad, *Das fünfte Buch Mose* (1964) 36.

[59]   Cf. D. Knapp, *Deuteronomium 4* (1987) 21–25.

[60]   For a summary, cf. *ibid.*, 112–113.

[61]   Cf. my "Literary critical studies of Deut 4", *Biblische Notizen* 81 (1996) 101, where I argue that there are other thematic changes within each of Knapp's other blocks, where the question of another author not even is discussed, even though these thematic changes probably could be said to be more significant than the change between vv. 9–14 and 15–16a*; cf. e.g. the reference to Baal Peor in the first block, v. 3, and the reference to the Exodus experience in the second block, v. 20.

[62]   Cf. G. Braulik, "Literarkritik und die Einrahmung vom Gemälden", *Revue Biblique* 96 (1989) 277–278.

this accent to the prohibition against making images.[63] Contrary to this I would argue that I find it difficult to see what the function of תמונה in v. 12 could be, if not to introduce the תמונה in vv. 15 ff. We have seen above that this noun is attested only ten times in the Old Testament; of which as many as six occurrences are found in Deuteronomy. Four of these are clear references to the Second commandment (4:16.23.25, 5:8). The fifth is just as clearly an introduction to one of these references (4:15); even in Knapp's system vv. 15 and 16a belong to the same text block. And the question is then if it really is reasonable that the sixth occurrence—the one here in v. 12—has a function that is totally independent of the others? In my opinion so is not the case. Besides this comes the fact that none of the four remaining Old Testament occurrences of תמונה outside Deuteronomy are used in a similar way, about something that is not seen. One is the Exodus version of the Second commandment, and the three others point out the תמונה as something that is positively seen. In other words, if the context of the תמונה in v. 12 is limited to vv. 9–14, this use of the word would have no parallels in the Old Testament.

One should therefore look for another explanation of the relationship between the two occurrences of תמונה in vv. 12 and 15. The noun תמונה obviously has the function of a terminological marker in vv. 15 ff.; together with other examples of central terminology of the Second commandment it links the passage to the commandment against images. And, I would say that תמונה has the same function already in v. 12. It certainly sticks out in the passage vv. 9–14;[64] however, the function of this is to signal a linking of this passage's focus on the verbal aspect of the Horeb theophany, the Decalogue, and its commandment against images. In other words, the noun תמונה in v. 12 makes completely sense when taken as a terminological marker preparing for the explicit bridging in vv. 15 ff. of the Horeb experience and the commandment against images.

---

[63]   D. Knapp, *Deuteronomium 4* (1987) 53, 179, n. 291.

[64]   Even D. Knapp, *Deuteronomium 4* (1987) 53, acknowledges this: "Diese Aussage setzt gegenüber dem Vorangegangenen einen neuen Akzent, der aber im folgenden zunächst nicht weiter ausgefürt wird."

Interpretive accent

What is then the interpretive accent of vv. 9–14's allusion to the Second commandment? The analysis of these verses has shown that this first passage of the core text of Deut 4 (vv. 9–31) emphasizes the verbal character of the Horeb theophany. Yahweh did not reveal himself through any visible "form" (תמונה), rather through the "sound of words" (קול דברים), and as a logical consequence of this, the covenant between Yahweh and Israel is identified as the verbally transmitted "ten words" (עשׂרת הדברים). When the following passages (vv. 15 ff.) narrow the focus from the Decalogue as a whole and to the Second commandment, this is prepared by the introduction of the terminological marker תמונה in v. 12. Far from being a random term chosen quite accidentally to express the non-visual emphasis of the Horeb theophany, the first passage's use of the marker תמונה is necessary for the next passage to relate the Horeb theophany and the Second commandment.

However, the marker תמונה in v. 12 has a broader function than simply to create a smooth transition from the Decalogue as a whole and to one particular of the commandments. More important is its function of providing a theological rationale of the following passages. Their focus on the Second commandment is presented as a logical consequence of the Horeb theophany, and the relationship between the theophany and the commandment is expressed through a conceptual parallelism. First, the noun תמונה is used by the first passage to point out the non-visual emphasis as the very center of the Horeb theophany. And secondly, when the following passages let this noun continue as a key word in the explicit allusions to the Second commandment, each of these allusions are related to this center of the Horeb theophany, thereby expressing an understanding of the Second commandment as the center of the Decalogue and main expression of the covenant. Accordingly, when Israel breaks the Second commandment, she violates the Horeb covenant and the Decalogue as a whole.

CHAPTER THREE

AN IMAGE, THE FORM OF ANY FIGURE

ANALYSIS OF VV. 15-16A

The previous chapter analyzed the focus of vv. 9–14 on the verbal character of the Horeb experience, and it was argued that the term תמונה serves as a marker, preparing for the present passage's linking of the verbal character of the Horeb theophany and the Second commandment's prohibition against making images.

(15) *Watch yourselves carefully, since you did not see any form on the day that Yahweh spoke to you at Horeb out of the midst of the fire;* (16) *beware so that you do not become corrupt and make for yourselves an image, the form of any figure, [...].*

Chapter 1 noticed some terminological markers in this passage, indicating a couple of allusions to the Second commandment:

תמונה	כל־	פסל	לך	תעשה־		לא־	C	5:8
תמונה	כל־				כי לא ראיתם	A	4:15b
תמונת כל־סמל		פסל	לכם	ועשיתם	פן־תשחתון	A	4:16a

A closer study of the passage reveals certain textual differences between the Decalogue version of the commandment and these allusions. One textual difference is the change of number between the addressees

of the two texts; the commandment has the singular תעשה־לך whereas v.
16a has plural ועשיתם לכם, cf. also the plurals of v. 15. Another textual
difference is the change of introductory negation; the commandment has
לא־, whereas v. 16a has פן־. Still, the major textual difference concerns
the expression כל־תמונה of the commandment, which is alluded to
verbatim in v. 15a, there, however, with a meaning apparently far away
from that of the commandment, as it is used to summarize the verbal
character of the Horeb theophany, whereas it is aluded to in passing as
תמונת כל־ in v. 16a, there with a meaning closely related to the
commandment.

Looking at these textual differences from the perspective of inner-
biblical interpretation, it seems reasonable to assume that they reflect and
express the interpretive accents of this passage vis-à-vis the Decalogue
version of the Second commandment. I will therefore use these
differences as an entry to a deeper understanding of the relationship
between the two texts, and the passage will be analyzed from the
following four perspectives: (1) the change of number, (2) the change of
negation, and (3) the inverted expressions תמונת כל־/כל־תמונה in vv. 15–
16a and their relationship to the כל־תמונה of the Decalogue version, and
(4) the interpretive accent of the allusions.

Change of number

An obvious difference between the Second commandment in its
Decalogue form in Deut 5:8 and the allusion here in Deut 4:16a is that
there is a change of number between the singular of the former, תעשה־לך,
and the plural of its rendering here in v. 16, ועשיתם לכם; cf. also the
plurals in v. 15. Clearly, change of number is by no means a surprise
within Deuteronomy; the frequent change of number throughout this
book has actually kept literary critics busy for more than a century, not
least with Deut 4.[65] Let me here confine myselt to make a few brief
comments to the fact that the different number between the Second
commandment in its Decalogue form and the three allusions here in Deut
4 has played a certain role also in the more general discussion about the
change of number in Deuteronomy.

---

[65]   For a brief survey, cf. my "Literary critical studies of Deut 4: Some
criteriological remarks", *Biblische Notizen* 81 (1996) 95–98.

According to C.T. Begg, the frequent change of number in Deut 4 could be explained as a result of deliberate quotations from older texts.[66] Begg proceeds from the concept that this chapter is a late synthesis of Deuteronomistic theology, and within this late synthesis the quotation model is put forward as one possible explanation of the frequent change of number. The author(s) of Deut 4 is (are) then argued to have switched to the plural or singular for a given formula, according to whether the formula in question customarily was cast in plural or singular in the Deuteronomistic texts with which he was familiar.[67] Begg argues that this model is of special relevance for vv. 9–24, which includes two of the three allusions to the Second commandment (vv. 16 and 23). These verses, according to Begg, constitute some kind of *relecture* of the Horeb account (and attached paraenesis) in Deut 5:1–6:1(3) and 9:7b–10:11, where phrases seem to have been taken over more or less verbally.[68]

Begg then examines the instances of change of number throughout vv. 1–40, and he is able to demonstrate a number of cases where the quotation model makes good sense.[69] However, when he comes to the triple allusion to the opening phrase of the Second commandment in vv. 16, 23, and 25, that is those instances throughout Deut 4 containing the theologically and even numerically most significant quotations, his quotation model turns out to be quite inadequate. The singular form of the Decalogue version of the commandment is in all three cases replaced by plural forms. Begg discusses the first quotation (v. 16), arguing that "[...] the number has been transposed into the plural of the context".[70] This is of course a reasonable argument, although it destroys the quotation model as such. More problematic, however, and unfortunately not discussed by Begg, are the two remaining quotations in vv. 23b and 25b. In those cases one can hardly say that the number has been transposed into the plural of the context, since the plural ועשׂיתם in both cases introduces the singular יהוה אלהיך.

---

[66] Cf. C.T. Begg, "The literary criticism of Deut 4,1–40. Contributions to a continuing discussion", *Ephemerides Theologicae Lovanienses* 56 (1980) 28–45.

[67] Cf. *ibid.*, p. 28.

[68] Cf. *ibid.*, p. 29.

[69] Cf. *ibid.*, pp. 29 ff.

[70] Cf. *ibid.*, p. 34.

Begg's suggestion has gained some support from D. Knapp,[71] as the concept of Deut 4 as a late paraenetic text, deliberately quoting older material, fits very well in with Knapp's basic understanding of this chapter.[72] However, when Knapp comes to vv. 16, 23, and 25, and their plural rendering of the Second commandment, the quotation model is not even being discussed. Actually, Knapp, who on the whole is very concerned with any question that could have literary critical significance, never analyzes this particular problem.[73] That is a pity, as such an analysis probably would have strengthened Knapp's criticism of the role that change of number traditionally has played in literary critical studies of Deuteronomy.

This obviously does not invalidate the concept of Deut 4 as a late parenetic text, deliberately reusing older material, such as for example the Second commandment. It just demonstrates that change of number hardly has any interpretive significance, even when it, as here in Deut 4, occurs in a text alluding to a highly esteemed text such as the Decalogue.

Change of negation

The second textual difference concerns the change of negation. The prohibitive form of the Second commandment in its Decalogue version, לא followed by *qal* imperfect of עשׂה, that is "you shall not make ..." (Deut 5:8), is in Deut 4:16a exchanged for the negative telic particle פן, followed by two verbs, *hiphil* imperfect of שׁחת and *qal* perfect of עשׂה, that is "so that you do not become corrupt and make ...".

The particle פן, which in most cases is rendered "lest" or "so that not", occurs five times in Deut 4, vv. 9.9.16.19.23. Three of these occurrences are directly linked to *niphal* imperatives of שׁמר, expressing a paraenetic warning: "Watch yourselves carefully ... so that you do not ..."; that is the השמר in v. 9, which governs the double פן...פן in the same verse, and also the השמרו in v. 23, governing the single פן. The two remaining ones, those in vv. 16 and 19, could seem to have a more

---

[71] Cf. D. Knapp, *Deuteronomium 4* (1987) 23: "Es ist damit zu rechnen, daß die spät-dtr Verfasser z.T. bewußt auch den Numerus übernahmen, wenn sie Passagen aus dem ihnen vorliegenden Material übernahmen."

[72] Cf. *ibid.*, p. 24.

[73] Cf. *ibid.*, pp. 69, 78–79, 82.

independent function, as they appear right at the beginning of a sentence.[74] However, also these two are preceded by a *niphal* form of שׁמר. And, as demonstrated by the table below, when it is read within the context of vv. 9 and 23, the *niphal* perfect ונשמרתם in v. 15 serves to introduce the פן...פן-sequence in vv. 16–19, a sequence where the פן in v. 16 and the ופן in v. 19 then create a parallelism between vv. 16–18 and 19.[75]

ופן	תשכח ...		פן	... לך	השמר	v. 9
					ונשמרתם	v. 15
... לכם פסל	ועשיתם		... פן			v. 16
		ופן				v. 19
... לכם פסל	ועשיתם	תשכחו ...	פן	לכם	השמרו	v. 23

The פן...ופן-sequence in vv. 16–19 continues the line of thought from v. 15, where two topics are being combined. First, in v. 15a, Israel is exhorted to be careful (cf. שׁמר), and then, in v. 15b, this exhortation is motivated (cf. כי) by a reference to the mode of the Horeb theophany.

The reference to the Horeb experience in v. 15b echoes the similar reference in v. 12. Still, the contextual function of the references to Horeb in vv. 12 and 15 is not exactly the same. Both clearly belong to a paraenetic context. However, whereas v. 12 is a part of broader and more narrative paraenesis (vv. 9–14), where the verbal aspect of the theophany is just one of several aspects of the Horeb experience that challenges Israel to follow Yahweh's decrees and laws, so does v. 15 link the verbal aspect of the theophany to one particular commandment, the prohibition against making images. By help of the particle פן a direct transition is made from the verbal aspect of the Horeb experience in v. 15b to the allusion to the Second commandment in v. 16a. Thereby the prohibition against making images is made the focus of the paraenesis.

---

[74] As for this initial position of פן, one could compare with the function of the double פן in Deut 29:17.

[75] The parallelling function of the פן...ופן-sequence in vv. 16 and 19 is acknowledged by recent commentators such as G. Braulik, *Die Mittel deuteronomischer Rhetorik* (1978) 37, 88–89; D. Knapp, *Deuteronomium 4* (1987) 69–72 (although he argues that vv. 16b–18 is a later addition, cf. below, pp. 54–63); and D.L. Christensen, *Deuteronomy 1–11* (1991) 86.

The particle פֶּן is generally used to express the idea of a warning; according to T. Muraoka it indicates "[...] a negative wish of a speaker".[76] The combination here in Deut 4 of פֶּן with a *niphal* of שׁמר, which expresses the idea of "to be on one's guard" or "to give attention to",[77] is frequently attested throughout Deuteronomy.[78] And when the allusion to the Second commandment here in v. 16a lets פֶּן substitute the לֹא of the Decalogue version of the commandment, its function is therefore simply to transform the prohibitive form of the Second commandment in its Decalogue version into the present paraenetic exposition of this commandment.

The inverted expressions כל־תמונה/תמונת כל־

A third textual difference between the Second commandment in its Decalogue form and the allusions here in Deut 4:15–16a, concerns the Decalogue expression כל־תמונה (Deut 5:8). This expression is first alluded to *verbatim* in v. 15, there, however in a context and with a meaning apparently far away from that of the commandment: it serves to summarize the focus of vv. 9–14 on the verbal aspect of the Horeb theophany. But then it is inverted and repeated as תמונת כל־ in v. 16a, there in a context and with a meaning closely related to the commandment: it serves to introduce the list of prohibited idols of vv. 16b–18.

	תמונה	כל־	פסל	C 5:8
	תמונה	כל־		A 4:15
סמל	כל־	תמונת	פסל	A 4:16a

The accumulation throughout Deut 4 of the noun תמונה has been discussed above, and it was argued that it already from v. 12 serves as a marker, preparing for v. 15's linking of the verbal aspect of the Horeb

---

[76]   Cf. P. Joüon & T. Muraoka, *A Grammar of Biblical Hebrew* (1991) 635.

[77]   Cf. F. García López, "שׁמר", *Theologisches Wörterbuch zum Alten Testament* 8 (1995) 303–304.

[78]   Cf. Deut 4:9.23, 6:12, 8:11, 11:16. 12:13.19.30, 15:9; cf. also M. Weinfeld, *Deuteronomy and the Deuteronomic School* (1972) 357.

theophany and the prohibition against making images.[79] Let us here, therefore, first turn our attention to its counterpart in the commandment expression כל־תמונה alluded to in both vv. 15 and 16a, the particle כל. After that we will turn to the extended expression פסל תמונת כל־סמל in v. 16a.

Throughout the Old Testament the major bulk of the כל occurrences appear in the construct state, and when—as is the case here in vv. 15–16a in both כל־תמונה and in the inverted תמונת כל־[סמל]—it appears as כל plus undetermined noun in singular, it should be translated with the indefinite and individualizing "any".[80] Now, Deuteronomy turns out to contain 353 of the total number of 5404 Old Testament occurrences of the particle כל.[81] This preference for כל has, as pointed out by H. Ringgren, a theological function, as it reflects Deuteronomy's interest for completeness.[82] When v. 15 places a כל in front of the תמונה of v. 12, it expresses this interest; the emphasizing of the verbal character of the Horeb theophany is strengthened from "you saw no form" in v. 12 to "you did not see *any* form" in v. 15. And, likewise, the כל־ in front of סמל in v. 16a acts as an emphasizing of the prohibition against making images, "an image, the form of *any* [...]".

However, when v. 15 places a כל in front of an echo of the תמונה of v. 12, it has also another function. What we have in v. 15 is certainly no

---

[79]   Cf. above, pp. 28–32.

[80]   For general surveys of the Old Testament use of כל, cf. H. Ringgren, "כל", *Theologisches Wörterbuch zum Alten Testament* 4 (1984) 145–153 (esp. cols. 145–146, with a discussion of different grammatical functions); and G. Sauer, "כל", *Theologisches Handwörterbuch zum Alten Testament* 1 (1984) 828–830.

[81]   There are 24 occurrences of כל in Deut 4; vv. 3, 4, 6, 7, 8, 9, 10, 15, 16, 17 (2x), 18 (2x), 19 (3x), 23, 25, 29 (2x), 30, 34, 40, 49. G. Braulik, *Die Mittel deuteronomischer Rhetorik* (1978) 127, n. 100, points out that within Deuteronomy only (the considerably longer) ch. 28 has more occurrences of כל than ch. 4.

[82]   Cf. H. Ringgren, "כל", *Theologisches Wörterbuch zum Alten Testament* 4 (1984) 149, who argues: "Im Deut haben die *kol*-Aussagen oft eine theologische Funktion. Der Himmel und die Erde und *alles*, was darauf ist, gehören JHWH (10,14), aber aus *allen* Völkern hat JHWH Israel erwählt (7,6 f. [...]), und nun soll Israel ihm lieben 'von *ganzem* Herzen, von *ganzer* Seele und mit *aller* seiner Kraft' (6,5; vgl. 10,12) und *alle* seine Gebote einhalten (11,8.22; 28,15; vgl. Ez 18,21)."

accidental combination of two casual terms, which then eventually in v. 16, and just as accidentally, are being inverted. On the contrary, when v. 15 uses the expression כל־תמונה to describe the Horeb theophany, it chooses an expression which occurs only twice elsewhere in the Old Testament, that is in the two Decalogue versions of the Second commandment, Deut 5:8 and Exod 20:4. And this connection is of course not accidental. Due to two of its three Old Testament occurrences, the expression כל־תמונה must surely be recognized as a theologically central term in the Old Testament prohibition against the making of images. As noticed above, the function of this expression here in v. 15 is to make possible the transition from the narrative about the Horeb theophany in v. 12 and to the more explicit allusion to the Second commandment in v. 16. Summarizing the Horeb experience, which *per se* has nothing to do with the Second commandment, v. 15 uses a terminology which inevitably leads the thoughts of the reader or listener to this very commandment, thereby preparing for the following verses.

When the expression כל־תמונה in v. 15 then re-occurs in the more explicit reference to the Second commandment in v. 16a, it has been inverted and extended. It has been inverted to תמונת כל־, and it has been extended by two more nouns, a preceding פסל and a following סמל. The introduction of the preceding noun פסל is quite easy to understand. Together with the noun תמונה and the verb עשה it is the clearest marker in this passage alluding to the Second commandment. The Old Testament usage of פסל can roughly can be divided in three.[83] It occurs (a) in texts expressing polemics against images, (b) in texts expressing polemics against non-yahwistic religion, and (c) in texts related to the Second commandment, as here in Deut 4. In all three areas the term פסל is traditionally translated "graven image",[84] as it is related to the verb פסל, "hew into shape".[85] However, C. Dohmen has convincingly shown that the aspect of how the פסל has been manufactured has lost its importance in the Old Testament texts, where it generally designates a cultic

---

[83]   For a survey, cf. C. Dohmen, "פסל", *Theologisches Wörterbuch zum Alten Testament* 6 (1989) 694–697.

[84]   This rendering is also reflected in recent translations of the Second commandment, as for example that of D.L. Christensen, *Deuteronomy 1– 11* (1991) 109, whereas for example M. Weinfeld, *Deuteronomy 1–11* (1991) 275, renders it with the less old-fashioned "carved image".

[85]   Cf. Exod 34:1.4, Deut 10:1.13, 1 Kings 5:32, Hab 2:18.

image.[86] The cultic aspect is of course obvious in the present context of the Second commandment, therefore I have translated פסל just as "image".

The inversion of v. 15's כל־תמונה to v. 16a's תמונת כל־ has rhetorical as well as syntactic functions.[87] From a rhetorical perspective, a parallel is created between v. 16a's תמונת כל־ [סמל] and the 4x [...] תבנית כל־ in vv. 17–18.[88] Thereby a link is created between v. 16a's prohibition against images, and vv. 17–18's list of imaginable images. And from a syntactic perspective, it creates an opening for linking the allusion to the Second commandment to the following noun סמל. What, then, is the function of this following noun סמל? The noun סמל occurs only five times in the Old Testament; Deut 4:16, Ezek 8:3.5, 2 Chron 33:7.15. From a syntactic point of view, we notice that only one of these references lets the סמל stand on its own (2 Chron 33:15), whereas the remaining four let it occur in construct chains; two where סמל is *nomen rectum* (Deut 4:16 and 2 Chron 33:7) and two where it is *nomen regens* (Ezek 8:3.5). Syntactically, 2 Chron 33:7 is therefore the closest parallel to Deut 4:16. These two texts are also the only ones directly linking סמל and פסל.

From a semantic point of view סמל has traditionally been rendered "figure" or "image".[89] This rendering, however, has in recent years been challenged by C. Dohmen. He argues that the Semitic root *sml*, which occurs only within the Phoenician/Punic and Hebrew areas, from an etymological point of view "[...] im Bereich der Bilderterminologie kein Wesens-, sondern ein funktionaler Begriff ist."[90] And further he claims "[...] daß der Begriff סמל immer von einem anderen, eigentlichen

---

[86]   Cf. C. Dohmen, "פסל", *Theologisches Wörterbuch zum Alten Testament* 6 (1989) 688–697; cf. also his "פסל—פסיל. Zwei Nominalbildungen von פסל?", *Biblische Notizen* 16 (1981) 11–12, and *Das Bilderverbot* (1987) 41–49.

[87]   Inversion is a frequently attested device within Hebrew poetry; for an introductory survey, cf. W.G.E. Watson, *Classical Hebrew Poetry* (1984) 356–359.

[88]   Cf. G. Braulik, *Die Mittel deuteronomischer Rhetorik* (1978) 40–41.

[89]   Cf. F. Brown & al., *The New Brown-Driver-Briggs-Gesenius Hebrew and English Lexicon* (1979) 702.

[90]   C. Dohmen, "Heißt פסל 'Bild, Statue'?", *Zeitschrift für die alttestamentliche Wissenschaft* 96 (1984) 263–266.

Bildbegriff her im Sinne eines beigestellten Kultobjekts definiert wird."[91]
Whatever the etymology of סמל might be, it still seems to me that its Old
Testament use defends the traditional rendering of something concrete,
such as an "image" or a "figure". Without such a rendering, the ואת־הסמל
in 2 Chron 33:15 would seem to require a closer definition, and so would
probably also the two *nomen regens* occurrences (סמל הקנאה) in Ezek
8:3.5. Here in Deut 4:16a the construct chain תמונת כל־סמל should
therefore be translated "the form of any figure".

V. 16a expresses the prohibition of making "an image, the form of
any figure". The function of the appositional relationship between פסל
and תמונת כל־סמל is of course to give a closer determination of the פסל.
But the two expressions are hardly synonyms. Whereas פסל, as just
pointed out, refers to the cultic image, and thereby concentrates on the
prohibition as such against making images, the appositional phrase
תמונת כל־סמל moves the interest in the direction of the different
expressions such images could have.[92] Logically, this prepares the reader
for vv. 16b–18, where such different expressions are being focused.

There is, however, another, and—in this context—often neglected
effect of the appositional phrase. It is clear from the other four Old
Testament occurrences of סמל that this noun has clear connotations of
non-yahwistic deities. 2 Chron 33 uses סמל twice to describe Manasseh's
relationship to the "detestable practices of the nations" (v. 2). Manasseh
is said to have followed these practices, and he is accused of placing the
פסל הסמל (v. 7) he had made in the temple in Jerusalem. Here we notice
that the parallel text in 2 Kings 21:7 identifies the deity, by reading

---

[91]   C. Dohmen, *Das Bilderverbot* (1987) 208. It should here be noticed that D.
       Knapp and C. Dohmen interpret the contextual function of סמל in Deut
       4:16 from the perspective that this word is a later addition, originating from
       the same hand as the following vv. 16b–18. Knapp points out (i) that the
       key expression תמונת כל reoccurs in vv. 23 and 25, there, however,
       without סמל, and (ii) that סמל elsewhere in the Old Testament is attested
       only in Ezek and 2 Chron, that is textual traditions closer to the
       (supposedly) Priestly origin of the immediately following vv. 16b–18. Cf.
       D. Knapp *Deuteronomium 4* (1987) 69–70; and C. Dohmen *Das
       Bilderverbot* (1987) 208–210. Their interpretation of vv.16b–18 as an
       addition will be challenged below, cf. pp. 54–69.

[92]   Cf. C. Dohmen, *Das Bilderverbot* (1987) 219.

פסל האשרה, "image of Ashera".[93] Also 2 Chron 33 identifies some of the non-yahwistic traits during the reign of Manasseh; he is accused of having "[...] erected altars to the Baals, and made Asherahs, and worshiped all the host of heaven, and served them" (v. 3). But then Manasseh, according to 2 Chron 33, humbled himself before "the God of his fathers" (v. 12), and started to clean the temple. Here the noun סמל re-occurs, when v. 15 in the description of how Manasseh gets rid of the idolatry in the temple makes a syntactic parallelling between the two expressions את־אלהי הנכר, "the foreign gods", and ואת־הסמל.

Also Ezek 8 uses סמל twice, vv. 3 and 5; both times in the expression סמל הקנאה, "image of jealousy". This expression is mostly taken as referring to the jealousy of Yahweh, provoked by the presence of an image—probably of Asherah—that is placed in the temple in Jerusalem.[94] Contrary to this, H.C. Lutzky has suggested that the הקנאה here should be taken as a form of קנה, "(pro)create", rather than of קנא, "be jealous". Instead of referring to the jealousy of Yahweh provoked by the סמל, it then, according to Lutzky, refers to the character of the actual deity, that is "Asherah the Creatress".[95] The traditional interpretation, however, is more convincing, partly because it reflects the general usage of the word קנאה in Ezekiel,[96] but partly also because the idea of Yahweh's jealousy is an important aspect of the Old Testament prohibition of images; cf. the אל קנא-texts related to the Second commandment, Deut 5:9/Exod 20:5 and Deut 4:24. Accordingly, in Ezek 8 the expression סמל הקנאה, as noticed by W. Zimmerli, then reflects Ezekiel's polemical description of the idolatry in the temple.[97]

---

[93] For an analysis of the development from פסל האשרה in 2 Kings 21:7 to פסל הסמל, in 2 Chron 33:7, cf. C. Frevel, "Die Elimination der Göttin aus dem Weltbild des Chronisten", *Zeitschrift für die alttestamentliche Wissenschaft* 103 (1991) 263–271.

[94] Cf. M. Greenberg, *Ezekiel 1–20* (1983) 168, who advocates the linking to Asherah, arguing that "It is fitting that this goddess's image should be referred to by the Phoenician/Canaanite *sml.*"

[95] Cf. H.C. Lutzky, "On 'the image of jealousy' (Ezekiel viii 3, 5)", *Vetus Testamentum* 46 (1996) 121–125.

[96] The word is used with Yahweh as acting subject in Ezek 5:13, 16:38.42, 23:25, 36:5.6, 38:19; the only exception is 35:11, where the acting subject is Mount Seir.

[97] Cf. W. Zimmerli, *Ezechiel 1–24* (1969) 212–215.

In other words, four of a total of five Old Testament occurrences of the noun סמל have clear connotations of non-yahwistic deities. It is then reasonable to argue that the same is also the case for the fifth, here in Deut 4:16a.

Interpretive accent

What is then the interpretive accent of vv. 15-16a's allusion to the Second commandment? The analysis of this passage has demonstrated that the first example of Deut 4's triple allusions to the introductory words of the Second commandment reflects an interpretation where the commandment is placed in a paraenetic context. Of particular interest in this interpretation is the relationship between the expression כל־תמונה, attested both in the Second commandment itself and here in v. 15, and then also in its inverted form, תמונת כל־, in v. 16a.

In the textual development of vv. 12 ff., the focus is on Yahweh and how he revealed himself at Horeb. As pointed out in the previous chapter, the very point here is that the theophany was a verbal one; Israel heard the voice of Yahweh, but she saw no תמונה. When v. 15 moves the attention in the direction of the Second commandment, by placing a כל־ in front of this תמונה, it is still Yahweh who is being focused; Israel did not see any תמונה of Yahweh at Horeb. Thus, the expression כל־תמונה in v. 15 prepares the reader for the Second commandment understood as a prohibition against making images of Yahweh. However, when v. 16a lets the כל־תמונה from v. 15—in its inverted form—be linked to the noun סמל, it suddenly opens up for an interpretation of the prohibition against making images that also relates it to images of non-yahwistic deities. The following passages will develop this new accent further.

• CHAPTER FOUR •

THE LIKENESS OF MALE AND FEMALE

ANALYSIS OF VV. 16B-18

After the explicit prohibition against any making of cultic images in v. 16a, and its theological legitimizing in v. 15, the next passage, vv. 16b–18, further develops this prohibition by turning the attention towards the variety in which such images can occur. And the text is utterly clear, it cannot imagine any kind of cultic images that are not included in the prohibition:

> (16) [...] the likeness of male or female, (17) the likeness of any animal that is on the earth, the likeness of any winged bird that flies in the sky, (18) the likeness of anything that creeps on the ground, the likeness of any fish that is in the waters below the earth.

Chapter 1 noticed some terminological markers in this passage, indicating a series of allusions to the Second commandment:

C 5:8aβ–b	אשר בשמים ממעל	ואשר בארץ מתחת	ואשר במים מתחת לארץ
A 4:17–18	אשר בארץ	אשר ... בשמים	אשר־ במים מתחת לארץ

As far as the use of these terminological markers is concerned, one notices clear similarities, such as the existence of three corresponding אשר-sentences in each passage, of which the last one in each case are identical, as well as differences, such as the order of the two first אֲשֶׁר-sentences. However, the passage consists of more than a series of אֲשֶׁר-sentences. I will argue in this chapter that the highly schematic form of this passage is made up by a combination of two schemes; one scheme that consists of 3x אֲשֶׁר-sentences, another that consists of 5x תבנית-sentences. The following outline of the text attempts to demonstrate the existence and relationship between these two schemes:

		זכר או נקבה	תבנית v. 16b
בארץ	אשר	כל־ בהמה	תבנית v. 17a
תעוף בשמים	אשר	כל־ צפור כנף	תבנית v. 17b
רמש באדמה		כל־	תבנית v. 18a
במים מתחת לארץ	אשר	כל־ דגה	תבנית v. 18b

Against this background, the passage will in the following be analyzed from four perspectives: (1) its style and structure, (2) the 5x תבנית-scheme, (3) the 3x אֲשֶׁר-scheme, and (4) the interpretive accent of the allusions.

Style and structure

The absolute rejection in vv. 16b–18 of making any kind of cultic images is expressed in a language that is characterized by a most conspicuous schematic style. Being organized as a series of parallel lines, together with a preference for verbal repetitions as well as a sensitivity for assonance and alliteration, this passage creates the impression of a sophisticated piece of literature.

The schematic style is recognized and emphasized as important by several recent commentators. However, it is comprehended quite differently; what is taken as "monoton, umständlich, formelhaft" by D. Knapp,[98] can be taken as "besonders effektvolles Stihlmittel" by G. Braulik.[99] Their different comprehension of the schematic style is probably, to some extent, a result of personal and subjective preferences vis-à-vis different literary expressions. But it also reflects their differing methodological approaches. On the one hand, Knapp's quite traditional

---

[98]   D. Knapp, *Deuteronomium 4* (1987) 89.

[99]   G. Braulik, *Die Mittel deuteronomischer Rhetorik* (1978) 42.

literary critical approach to Deut 4 makes him look for features in the text that result from its (supposed) growth. With regard to vv. 16b–18 this approach leads Knapp to argue that the schematic style reflects that the passage is a later addition, originating from a "hand" with other literary ideals than the "hand" (or "hands") responsible for the surrounding verses. By contrast, Braulik's more literary approach to Deut 4, which makes him sensitive to all kinds of rhetorical and stylistic features, leads him to argue that the schematic style of vv. 16b–18 reflects its rhetorical and contextual function. The two approaches, however, are not necessarily mutually exclusive, and insights from both will be reflected in the following analysis.

The outline above of the text demonstrates that the passage is structured as a repetition of parallel lines. In its full form the line consists of an apposition and a relative clause. The apposition consists of the noun תבנית plus a specification, the latter introduced by an indefinite כל־. The relative clause is introduced by אשר, which is followed by a spatial placing, the latter introduced by the preposition ב plus the definite article. Nevertheless, and in spite of what this passage is able to demonstrate of a rather strict structure of verbal repetition and parallel lines, it also reveals some surprising gaps. The co-existence of this strict structure together with the surprising gaps deserves some comments.

Let us first look at vv. 16b–18 from a point of view that acknowledges its strict structure. Not least G. Braulik has emphasized that the stylistic function of the 5x introductory תבנית is to introduce the repetitive pattern of the passage.[100] Repetition is a very frequently attested literary device in Deuteronomy. And here in Deut 4 it occurs in many different forms, such as for example the 4x negation (לא) plus verb (all in *qal* imperfect, 3rd person plural, with *nun paragogicum*) in v. 28b,[101] or the two parallel rhetorical מי־questions opening vv. 7 and 8.[102] However, an even closer parallel to the 5x תבנית here in vv. 16b–18 is the 5x ארץ in Deut 8:7b–9:

---

[100]   *Ibid.*, 42.

[101]   Also in v. 28b this repetition serves to give a description of images: "wood and stone, that neither see (לא יראון), nor hear (ולא ישמעון), nor eat (ולא יאכלון), nor smell (ולא יריחן)".

[102]   The two questions are terminologically almost identical:

     v. 7aα   כי מי־גוי גדול אשר־לו [...]

     v. 8aα ו-   מי גוי גדול אשר־לו [...]

טובה	אל־ ארץ	כי יהוה אלהיך מביאך	v. 7a
	ארץ נחלי מים		v. 7b
	ארץ חטה ושערה		v. 8a
	ארץ־זית שמן		v. 8b
	ארץ		v. 9a
	ארץ		v. 9b
הטבה	על־ הארץ	וברכת את־יהוה אלהיך	v. 10b

The structuring of Deut 8:7b–9, 5x ארץ plus further specification, framed
by the ארץ טובה in vv. 7a and 10, is a parallel to 4:16b–18 also as both
express the specification in terms of an appositional relationship.[103] I will
soon come back to this text from Deut 8.

The introductory repetition of תבנית in 4:16b–18 is then, to some
extent, followed by the rest of the five lines; in four of the lines the
repetitive pattern is expressed by a כל־ plus specification, and in three of
the lines it is expressed by אשר-sentences. The function of this repetition
of parallel lines could be manifold, as repetition indeed has several
different functions within Hebrew prose and poetry.[104] W.G.E. Watson
has, in general terms, pointed out three different functions; first, that
repetition enables the audience to re-hear a verse which they may have
missed, further that it reduces the need for an author to invent new
material, and finally that it helps to link the components of a passage.[105]
The two former explanations are hardly appropriate here in vv. 16b–18.
Missing a line would actually prevent an audience listening to this
passage from grasping the full meaning of it, and there are no signs that

---

[103]   The rhetorical function of Deut 8:7b–9, within the larger structure of vv. 1–
20, is expounded by R.H. O'Connell, "Deuteronomy viii 1–20:
Asymmetrical concentricity and the rhetoric of providence", *Vetus
Testamentum* 40 (1990) 437–452; this article develops ideas expressed
already by N. Lohfink, *Das Hauptgebot* (1964) 189–199.

[104]   I will not go into any discussion of whether vv. 16b–18 should be labelled
'prose' or 'poetry'; in my opinion the two are not mutually exclusive, cf.
the discussion of that topic in the excursus "Prose or poetry?" in my *Second
Isaiah's Idol-fabricating Passages* (1995) 207–212. Still, I basically agree
with D.L. Christensen's view that most of Deut could be called "didactic
poetry"; cf. his *Deuteronomy 1–11* (1991) lv–lxii, and his "Prose and
poetry in the Bible. The narrative poetics of Deuteronomy 1,9–18",
Zeitschrift für die alttestamentliche Wissenscaft 97 (1985) 179–189.

[105]   W.G.E. Watson, *Classical Hebrew Poetry* (1984) 278–279.

the author lacked material. The third explanation, that is the suggestion that repetition helps to link the components of the passage together, is better, as it points out a feature obviously delimiting the passage from its textual surroundings. Or, in other words, it seems to be an important function of the repetitive pattern of vv. 16b–18 that it delimits these verses as a distinct textual unit.

Closely related, but still to be distinguished from the stylistic function of the structure of vv. 16b–18, is the question of how this structure also reflects the theology of the passage. The passage on the benefits of the land in Deut 8:7b–9, pointed out above as a structural parallel to vv. 16b–18, can throw some light also on the theological implications of the structure here in vv. 16b–18. The passage in Deut 8 has a frame that relates the land to Yahweh. First, in vv. 6–7a, where the idea that Yahweh has brought Israel *to* the good land (אל־ארץ טובה) is used to challenge the people to obey Yahweh's commandments.[106] And then, in v. 10, where the people is challenged to praise Yahweh *because of* the good land (על־הארץ הטבה) they have been given. Thus, in Deut 8 stylistic features such as the repetition and initial position of the key word ארץ in vv. 7b–9 serves to accentuate the theology of the passage.

In the same way, I would argue, the 5x repetition of the introductory תבנית in Deut 4:16b–18 reflects what that passage is all about. Even G. Braulik, the foremost exponent for a stylistic analysis of Deut 4, who has often been accused of neglecting the theological implications reflected in the style and structure of a certain passage,[107] can argue that the introductory 5x תבנית serve to emphasize to the reader or listener the main topic of vv. 16b–18.[108] This passage focuses on the variety with

---

[106]   The כי in v. 7a is then taken as having the causal function "for", cf. R.H. O'Connell, "Deuteronomy viii 1–20: Asymmetrical concentricity and the rhetoric of providence", *Vetus Testamentum* 40 (1990) 443, n. 15; whereas some interpreters would give it the temporal function "when", cf. N. Lohfink, *Das Hauptgebot* (1964) 192; and A.D.H. Mayes, *Deuteronomy* (1979) 191.

[107]   Cf. e.g. S. Herrmann, "[Rec. of] G. Braulik, *Die Mittel deuteronomischer Rhetorik*", *Theologische Revue* 77 (1981) 10–12.

[108]   G. Braulik, *Die Mittel deuteronomischer Rhetorik* (1978) 42: "Fünfmal kehrt die Wendung *tabnît* (*kol*) wieder, wird also mit starker Emphase, die durch die Stellung dieser Phrase stets zu Zeilenbeginn nochmals gesteigert ist, dem Gedächtnis eingehämmert." Braulik also finds a similar link between style and theological accent with regard to the 4x negation (לא) + verb in v. 28b (cf. above, where I compared the style in this verse with that

which the prohibited images can occur, and this is what is being expressed by the initial repetition of the key word תבנית.

The function of the following appositions and relative clauses—in the full form of the line—is to give a closer definition of the תבנית. First, the appositions present a wide range of possible models for the תבנית: human beings, animals, birds, creeping things, and fish.[109] And then, the relative clauses localize these models: on earth, in the sky, on the ground, and in the water.

Now, let us leave the full form of the repetitive structure of vv. 16b–18, and proceed to its peculiar gaps. The first gap is found already in the opening line, v. 16b. Compared with the four others, this first line lacks the indefinite כל־ before the specification of תבנית through the word pair נקבה / זכר, and it also lacks the relative pronoun אשר plus a spatial placing after this specification. This structural disturbance, together with the initial position of the נקבה / זכר in the series of specifications, can probably be said to emphasize the importance of this word pair.

A more surprising gap in the repetitive structure of vv. 16b–18, as it seems to me, concerns v. 18a. Here the noun רמש (or an equivalent) is lacking; instead the verb (participle) רמש occurs, as a parallel to the verb עוף in v. 17b.[110] Lacking in v. 18a is also the relative pronoun אשר. The lacking noun and relative pronoun in v. 18a reveals a tension between the

---

of vv. 16b–18): "Das viermal wiederholte lōʾ hämmert dem Gedächtnis das totale Unvermögen dieser Götter ein. Aber auch der Gleichklang der Verben im emphatischen Afformativ -*ûn* und Präformativ *j* unterstreicht das Unisono der Unfähigkeit der auf ihre Bilder reduzierten Gottheiten zu alltäglich banalen und bloß menschlichen Handlungen."; *ibid.* p. 56.

[109]   It should here be noticed that the 5x תבנית in vv. 16b–18 only refer to "earthly" entities; the moon and the stars referred to in v. 19 are introduced in a different way, cf. below, ch. 5.

[110]   In D. Knapp's outline of the parallel structures in vv. 16b–18, *Deuteronomium 4* (1987) 89, the participle רמש is taken as a parallel to the nouns צפור, בהמה, and דגה. This interpretation, which emphasizes the nominal aspects of the participle, is possible. However, taking into consideration the close relationship between these verses and Gen 1:26–27 (cf. below), where the full expression is noun plus participle of the root רמש, I would tend to think that it has a verbal function alkso here in 4:18, and I have therefore placed it as a parallel to v. 17's עוף. This corresponds with the Septuagint rendering of the sentence. Still, in the end, on the consonant-level there is no difference between the participle and noun.

fourfold pattern related to כל־ and the threefold pattern related to אשׁר:[111]
v. 18a has both the indefinite כל־ and a spatial placing (אדמה plus the
preposition ב, as the three other כל־-sentences), but its lacking noun and
pronoun destroy the completeness of the parallelisms of vv. 17–18. It can
hardly be a means of emphasizing the (supposedly lacking noun) רמשׁ, as
is the case with the נקבה / זכר in v. 16b. I will come back to this problem
below.

What, then, is the function and background of the style and structure
in this passage? It is here necessary to develop an explanation that takes
into account both the strict schematic structure and the surprising gaps in
the same structure. I believe that the key to a proper understanding of the
structure of this passage lies in accepting the surprising gaps as reflecting
a deliberate construction rather than an accidental one. G. Braulik is
probably right when he, in connection with the lacking relative clause in
v. 18a, points out that in a structurally schematic text like vv. 16b–18 any
variation is of importance.[112] I will therefore suggest that the function of
the surprising gaps is to be textual signs, deliberately left in the passage
as reminders to the reader or listener that this passage is made up as a
combination of two different schemes: one is what I will call the אשׁר-
scheme, consisting of 3x אשׁר plus spatial placing, the other is what I will
call the תבנית-scheme, consisting of 5x תבנית plus a list specifications.
These two schemes could of course have been worked better together.
And the interpretation history shows examples of harmonizations. The
lacking אשׁר in v. 18a could easily have been placed in,[113] so could
clearly also a noun רמשׁ (or equivalent) besides the MT participle רמשׁ,[114]
and also v. 16b could have been more streamlined. Still, this is not done,
and the gaps stick out in an otherwise extremely strict structure. But

---

[111] This tension is also noticed by G. Braulik, *Die Mittel deuteronomischer
Rhetorik* (1978) 42.

[112] Cf. *ibid.*, 43.

[113] As it is done in the renderings of v. 18 in Targum Onkelos:

v. 18a	דמות כל רחשא	ד-בארע־
v. 18b	דמות כל נוני	ד-במיא מלרע לארעא

Notice here that the same harmonizing tendency is also reflected in its 2x
ארע (cf. also v. 17a) in v. 18 instead of MT's אדמה (v. 18a) and ארץ (v.
18b).

[114] As it is done in the Septuagint, which in v. 18a reads ὁμοίωμα παντὸς
ἑρπετοῦ ὃ ἕρπει ἐπὶ τῆς γῆς.

then, I would argue, these gaps have a fuction of their own. And this function is to make the reader or listener comprehend the interpretive accent of the passage, by recognizing the two schemes it is made up of. Let us therefore first go into each of the two schemes, respectively, and then look for the interpretive accent of the combination of the two schemes.

The תבנית-scheme

Let us start with the תבנית-scheme, which consists of 5x תבנית plus a list of specifications. The noun תבנית means a "figure" or "likeness", and its semantic emphasis is a resemblance between this figure and some particular original. Against this background it is understandable that the 20 Old Testament occurrences of תבנית have a broad range of usages, of which "idol" or "image" in the context of religious polemics is one.[115] The aspect of resemblance, however, is important here too. One example is Isa 44:13, where the point is that the idol is made according to "the likeness of a man (כתבנית איש)". Another example is Ps 106:20, where the point is that the Golden calf is made according to "the likeness of a bull (בתבנית שור) that eats grass".[116] And a third example is our passage, Deut 4:16b–18, where תבנית's aspect of resemblance has two important consequences. First, it fits well to its contextual function of exemplifying the preceding expression כל־סמל תמונת. And secondly, better than more explicit idol terminology, it is able to continue the preceding passage's focus on both yahwistic and non-yahwistic images. The images that are described in vv. 16b–18 could, in principle, be images of Yahweh; however, both the accumulative force of the various images and the preceding סמל point in the direction of non-yahwistic images.

As for the more general choice of terminology in the תבנית-scheme, it seems to indicate that we here deal with another literary tradition than what is reflected in its more typically Deuteronomistic context. Terms like the word pair זכר and נקבה, but also the series of the four kinds of living beings דגה, רמש, צפור כנף בהמה, and possibly even the noun תבנית, reminds one of the Priestly tradition rather than of the Deuteronomistic tradition.

---

[115]   For a survey, cf. S. Wagner, "בנה", *Theologisches Wörterbuch zum Alten Testament* 1 (1973) 704–706.

[116]   Cf. K. Holter, *Second Isaiah's Idol-fabrication Passages* (1995) 164–165.

This terminological feature was noticed by interpreters of Deut 4 more than a century ago, and the positions that were outlined in the latter half of the 19th century are still, more or less, relevant in the discussion. On the one hand A. Kuenen argued that the supposed Priestly terminology in vv. 16–18, together with other similar examples from throughout Deut 4, simply reflects that Deut 1:6–4:40 origins in exilic times, and "[...] is issued from Ezekiel's circle".[117] On the other hand, however, W. Staerk argued that the Priestly terminology in vv. 16b–18 rather reflects that vv. 15 ff. is a later addition to the context of vv. 10 ff.[118] Throughout the century that has passed since Kuenen and Staerk published their commentaries, most commentators have tended to ignore the resemblance between vv. 16b–18 and the Priestly literary tradition.[119] In recent years, however, the issue has again received some attention, and the most detailed and thorough contribution, which also summarizes the discussion up till the early 1980s, is D. Knapp's monograph on Deut 4.

---

[117] A. Kuenen, *An Historico-Critical Inquiry into the Origin and Composition of the Hexateuch* (1886) 336–337. According to Kuenen, the points of contact with the Priestly tradition are more numerous in Deut 4:1–40 than in any other part of Deuteronomy.

[118] W. Staerk, *Das Deuteronomium* (1894) 79, n. 3.

[119] This, of course, concerns the large number of superficial and devotional commentaries that has been and still is on the market. However, and at first sight this comes as a surprise, it also concerns a number of commentaries with a strong historical-critical profile. It seems to me that the interpretation history of vv. 16b–18 provides a good example of what historical criticism has often been accused of, namely a tendency of analysing various circumstances around (or behind) the texts, rather than the texts themselves. Generally speaking, it seems that the interpretation history of this text reveals a stronger interest for the possible references in the text to the religio-historical context of its author or intended audience, than for the text itself. An early and illustrative example of this is S.R. Driver, *A Critical and Exegetical Commentary on Deuteronomy* ([1895] 1978[3]) 69–70, who is familar with Kuenen's commentary (cf. p. xxvi), but whose focus still lies in the religio-historical background of what this text says about idolatry; hence his several literary references to comparative material on "animal worship" and totemism in early Arabia. The same tendency can be found in a large number of historical critical commentaries throughout the 20th century. Still, there are exceptions from this general tendency, and some of these will be referred to in the discussion below.

According to Knapp, the idea expressed in v. 12, that Israel saw no
תמונה during the Horeb theophany, is taken up by the later "hand" that
added vv. 15–16a*+19–28, and here it is developed into a major motive.
Since Israel saw no תמונה at Horeb, she should not make cultic images in
the תמונה of any creature. And then, yet another "hand" added vv. 16b*–
18 to vv. 15–16a*+19–28. The function of this addition is to describe the
various expressions the making of an image could mean. And this
"hand" uses a termonology that reflects familiarity with the Priestly
literary tradition:[120]

> Dem im Bereich der priesterschriftlichen Literatur beheimateten
> Ergänzer reicht die offene Formulierung des ihm vorliegende Textes
> nicht aus. Er ist der Auffassung, in dieser Sache müsse gründlicher
> und audführlicher geredet werden.[121]

Knapp's advocacy of a Priestly background of vv. 16b–18 is built upon
two sets of thought-lines: (i) the strikingly schematic structure is argued
to reflect a typical Priestly style, and (ii) so is also the choice of
terminology.

(i) With regard to his first argument—the strikingly schematic
structure—Knapp is certainly right in pointing out that vv. 16b–18
stylistically stick out vis-à-vis its close context. However, this does not
mean that also the conclusions he draws from this necessarily are correct.

First, Knapp claims that the schematic style of vv. 16b–18 reflects a
"hand" later than the one responsible for the surrounding vv. 15–16a and
19–28. Against this one could argue that Knapp here presupposes a very
limited literary freedom of each of the different "hands". The shift of
style between this passage and its surroundings could have other
explanations than the genetic one advocated by Knapp. A rival
explanation could be that of Braulik, who, as pointed out above,
emphasizes stylistic rather than genetic aspects.[122] Although Braulik, in
my opinion, generally exaggerates the occurrence of deliberate stylistic
means in Deut 4, I would tend to agree with him in this particular case.

---

[120] D. Knapp, *Deuteronomium 4* (1987) 88–91 and 112–114.

[121] *Ibid.*, 90.

[122] G. Braulik, *Die Mittel deuteronomischer Rhetorik* (1978) 42: "Der
Aufzählung der einzelnen körperhaften Wesen entspricht die Redefigur der
Asyndese als besonders effektvolles Stilmittel, zumal in einem Text, für
den sonst die Syndese charakteristisch ist."

And secondly, Knapp claims that this later hand responsible for the schematic style of vv. 16b–18 origins within Priestly circles. Quoting R. Smend, who describes the Priestly style as "monoton, umständlich, formelhaft",[123] Knapp points out the strong parallelistic structures of vv. 17–18, in which he recognizes this Priestly style.[124] Against this one could argue that the same of course could be said about the Deuteronomistic style. And since Knapp uses Smend to verify his description of the Priestly style, one should remember that Smend also acknowledges "die schematisch-rhetorische Struktur der dt Rede".[125] It should also be noticed that the Deuteronomistic tradition actually seems able to come up with structures which more or less correspond with those in vv. 16b–18. One could here—again (cf. above, p. 50)—compare with the 5x ארץ plus further specification in Deut 8:7b–9, a text that most scholars would characterize as typical Deuteronomistic.[126] From a structural point of view, the two passages are quite parallel, and I cannot see any fundamental differences between the 5x תבנית-scheme here in vv. 16b–18, and the 5x ארץ-scheme in ch. 8. Another example of the strict structure of vv. 16b–18 is the gender-matched parallelisms in vv. 17–18. Here, one could find corresponding structures even within the same chapter, and this in a verse which also Knapp takes as belonging to the Deuteronomistic tradition:[127] compare the f + f ‖ m + m pattern of v. 17 (שמים + צפור ‖ ארץ + בהמה) and the m + f >< f + m pattern of v. 18 (רמש + מים + דגה >< אדמה + ארץ ‖ שמים) with the m + m ‖ f + f pattern of v. 36abα (שמים + אש ‖ ארץ + קל).[128]

I would, accordingly, warn against drawing lines too quickly from the strikingly schematic style of vv. 16b–18 and to the question of the authorship of this passage. Although the schematic style clearly sticks out within the close literary context, I find it problematic to give these stylistic features genetic explanations. Other types of arguments are needed.

---

[123] R. Smend, *Die Entstehung des Alten Testaments* (1981²) 49.

[124] D. Knapp, *Deuteronomium 4* (1987) 89.

[125] R. Smend, *Die Entstehung des Alten Testaments* (1981²) 74.

[126] Cf. e.g. M. Weinfeld, *Deuteronomy and the Deuteronomic School* (1972) 172, 343.

[127] Cf. D. Knapp, *Deuteronomium 4* (1987) 106–107, 113.

[128] To the phenomenon of gender-matched parallelism, cf. W.G.E. Watson, *Classical Hebrew Poetry* (1984) 47 and 367.

(ii) And other types of arguments are certainly also available. Turning to Knapp's second argument—the choice of terminology—it is clear that a substantial part of vv. 16b–18 turns out to be made up by a terminology which elsewhere in the Pentateuch is reflected in texts generally attributed to the Priestly, rather that the Deuteronomistic tradition. First and foremost this concerns the word pair זכר and נקבה, but one notices also the series of the four creatures דגה, רמש, צפור כנף בהמה, and possibly even the noun תבנית.

As pointed out above, the peculiar terminology of vv. 16b–18, and also its possible affinities with the Priestly tradition, has been noticed by scholars for more than a century. Knapp, however, has developed the idea of a Priestly terminology into a model of textual growth in Deut 4. Arguing that there is a clear difference between vv. 16b–18, where one finds "Begriffe und Wendungen, die sonst für den priesterlichen Sprachgebrauch typisch sind", and their context, where one finds "im wesentlichen Begriffe und Wendungen aus dem dtr/spät-dtr Bereich",[129] he develops the terminological variation into a major argument in his claim that vv. 16b–18 is the work of a later hand, originating in Priestly circles.[130]

This calls for several remarks. Let it first be noticed that a linking between the particular terminology of vv. 16b–18 and the Priestly tradition concerns only half of the passage, i.e. the תבנית-scheme, and not necessarily the אשר-scheme (cf. more below). Secondly, and methodologically more problematic, is it that Knapp, as he emphasizes the occurrences of the terminology in question within texts from the Priestly tradition, in practice tends to overlook their—although fewer—occurrences within the non-Priestly and Deuteronomistic traditions. A survey of the distribution of the terminology in question should demonstrate this.[131]

---

[129]   D. Knapp, *Deuteronomium 4* (1987) 88–89.

[130]   *Ibid.*, 88–90.

[131]   The source analytical data in this survey follows F.I. Andersen & A.D. Forbes, *The Vocabulary of the Old Testament* (1992): תבנית (p. 443), זכר (p. 311), נקבה (p. 379), בהמה (p. 288), צפור (p. 407), רמש (p. 230), and דג/דגה (p. 77). The source analysis of Andersen & Forbes (see p. 7) follows O. Eissfeldt, *Hexateuch-Synopse* (1922), with its traditional wellhausenian sources: J, E, D, and P, and further Eissfeldt's L (= Lay source) and H (Holiness Code, Lev 17–26). Taking into account the uncertainty of traditional source analysis in contemporary Pentateuch scholarship, I prefer

	Tetrateuch		Deuteronomistic History (DH)		
	Non-Priestly	Priestly	Deut 4:16b-18	Rest of Deut	Rest of DH
תבנית		3	5		2
זכר	8	46	1	1	7
נקבה	2	18	1		
בהמה	25	61	1	16	10
צפור	1	14	1	2	
רמש	3	20	1		1
דג/דגה	4	3	1		1

From this survey it is clear that Knapp basically is right in connecting vv. 16b–18, or at least the תבנית-scheme, to the Priestly tradition. However, a closer study of the textual material will modify the picture somewhat. The list of the תבנית-scheme—consisting of various kinds of living beings belonging to heaven, earth and water—has a number of parallels throughout the Old Testament. The majority of these lists are found in the Tetrateuch,[132] but there is also one additional example in the Deuteronomistic History,[133] and some few scattered around elsewhere in

---

to talk about texts belonging to a "Priestly" (= P and H) or a "non-Priestly" (= J, L, and E) traditon—in addition to texts belonging to the Deuteronomistic tradition.

[132] There are fourteen relevant texts in the Tetrateuch, and these can be divided in three groups: 1) Two lists occur in connection with the creation of man in Gen 1:26–27.28. These two very close texts have the same order, but to some extent they vary with regard to terminology: the בהמה of v. 26 is lacking in v. 28. 2) As many as ten lists belong to the Noah narrative: Gen 6:7.20, 7:8.14.21.23, 8:17.19, 9:2.10. These lists, which—according to traditional source analysis—belong both to the Priestly and Non-Priestly traditions, describe the beings that were to be drowned or saved in the flood. Compared to most of the parallel lists, the ones in the Noah narrative, for obvious reasons, do not include references to fish—with the of exception 9:2, which refers to (1:26–27.28 and) the situation after the flood. 3) Two lists occur in Leviticus' discussion of clean and unclean animals: Lev 11:46 and 20:25.

[133] The only parallel in the Deuteronomistic History to the list in Deut 4:16b–18 is found in 1 Kings 5:13 [ET 4:33], that is a list belonging to a context that describes King Solomon's wisdom: "He also taught about animals and birds, reptiles and fish".

the Old Testament.[134] The following ones are those that are closest to the list in vv. 16b–18:

Gen 1:26–27 (P)	Gen 6:7 (Non–P)	Gen 9:2 (P)	Deut 4:16b–18 (DH)	1 Kings 5:13 (DH)
זכר/נקבה	אדם		זכר/נקבה	
דגה	בהמה	חית הארץ	בהמה	בהמה
עוף	רמש	עוף	צפור	עוף
בהמה	עוף	אשר תרמש כל	רמש	רמש
רמש		דג	דגה	דג

This outline should suffice to demonstrate that the list in vv. 16b–18 belongs to a textual tradition of lists presenting various kinds of living beings that belong to heaven, earth and water. Within this tradition, however, there is some variation with regard to both order and terminology. With regard to order, the closest parallel to the list in vv. 16b–18 is the single example from the Deuteronomistic History, 1 Kings 5:13; even the typical Priestly texts Gen 1:26–27 and 9:2 do not have the same order. And with regard to terminology, v. 17's צפור is very seldomly found within these lists, the favourite term for "bird" is עוף; within the Tetrateuch (and the Deuteronomistic History) צפור reoccurs only in in Gen 7:14.[135] However, the most important observation this outline invites us to do, from a terminological point of view, concerns vv. 16b–18's initial word pair זכר/נקבה: the non-Priestly Genesis example of this outline, Gen 6:7, includes "mankind" (אדם) in its list, but it is only the Priestly Gen 1:26–27 which—as the only list besides Deut 4:16b–18—includes the word pair זכר/נקבה. In other words, the closest terminological parallel to vv. 16b–18 is found in a Priestly text describing the creation of man.

---

[134] Of relevant lists outside both Tetrateuch and Deuteronomistic History, see Pss 8:8–9, 148:10, Hos 2:20 and 4:3, Ezek 38:20, Zeph 1:3.

[135] And this particular phrase where צפור occurs in Gen 7:14 is not very strong from a textual critical point of view, as it is lacking in the Septuagint and in some Hebrew manuscripts; see C. Westermann, *Genesis 1–11* (1974) 527. However, it should be noticed that צפור reoccurs in the two lists that were found in the Psalms; see Pss 8:9 and 148:10.

It should be clear that I find D. Knapp's terminological analysis very stimulating. However, in the end, I must admit that I am a bit ambivalent to his results. On the one hand, I find that Knapp too quickly moves from the observation that vv. 16b–18 reflect a typical Priestly terminology to the conclusion that the verses therefore reflect a textual growth. Knapp's genetic model leads him to exaggerate the Priestly features in vv. 16b–18, in order to make these features strong enough to justify the passage as an addition. Still, on the other hand, I would argue that Knapp does not go far enough in identifying the Priestly elements as reflecting a relationship between Deut 4 and one particular area of the Priestly literary tradition, its concept of creation.

Let us therefore take a closer look at the relationship between our passage and Gen 1. Two points should be made here. First, one should consider a suggestion made by M. Fishbane, that the series of objects of worship in vv. 16b–19a corresponds, in reverse order, with the list of the elements of creation in Gen 1.[136] Fishbane's suggestion is echoed in some subsequent commentaries, such as those by A.D.H. Mayes and C.J. Labuschagne,[137] and it is explicitly approved by a few other researchers, most recently by E. Otto.[138] If this suggestion, which links v. 19a to the preceding vv. 16b–18, is correct, it would complicate Knapp's interpretation of vv. 16b–18. On the one hand it would contradict Knapp's delimitation of vv. 16b–18 as a later addition, but on the other hand it would not necessarily contradict what Knapp claims to be the

---

[136] Cf. M. Fishbane, "Varia Deuteronomica", *Zeitschrift für die alttestamentliche Wissenschaft* 84 (1972) 349–352. This early study provides a good example of what Fishbane was later to develop into the concept of "inner-biblical exegesis"; cf. his "Inner-Biblical Exegesis", *Hebrew Bible / Old Testament* (1996) 33–48. The incipient attempts from 1972 related to Deut 4 are to some extent further elaborated in Fishbane's major study *Biblical Interpretation in Ancient Israel* (1985), cf. pp. 321–322.

[137] Cf. A.J.H. Mayes, *Deuteronomy* (1979) 153–154; and also C.J. Labuschagne, *Deuteronomium IA* (1987) 263. Mayes only claims this, whereas Labuschagne provides the details: "Deut. 4: *mensen, vee, vogels, kruipenden, vissen*. Gen 1: "*waterwezens*, vogels, wild vee, kruipenden, *mensen*". It should be noticed that neither of the two commentators refers explicitly to Fishbane.

[138] Cf. E. Otto, *Das Deuteronomium im Pentateuch und Hexateuch* (2000) 168–169; cf. also *idem*, "Deuteronomium 4", T. Veijola (ed.), *Das Deuteronomium und seine Querbeziehungen* (1996) 218–219.

Priestly character of vv. 16b–18, it would only extend it to v. 19a. However, a closer study shows that Fishbane and his followers are not very precise in their comparison of the two lists.[139] One thing is that both terminology and order differ, even within the two sets of listing (deliberation, creation) in the Genesis text; compare for example terminology and order in vv. 20/21 and 24/25. Another thing is that this makes it difficult to draw any exact lines between the Genesis text and Deut 4. Against this background I doubt that Fishbane is right when he claims that "Gen. 1 serves as the literary model for the speaker or writer."[140] However, this does not mean that there is no relationship between the two texts; even though there is no large scale chiasm between Gen 1 and Deut 4:16b–19a, there is still the small scale parallelism between Deut 4:16b–18 and Gen 1:26 f. that was pointed out above. These two lists are the only one in the Old Testament that include both the male/female part and the fourfold listing of animals, birds and fish, although the order of the fourfold listing is not the same.[141]

Secondly, I would like to emphasize that there are more examples within Deut 4 of a terminology one knows from Gen 1 in particular, and the Priestly tradition in general, than those in vv. 16b–18.[142] As pointed out above, some single words were noticed already a century ago by Kuenen and Staerk. And in the meantime there are other interpreters who have argued in the same direction. One example of a very influental interpreter of Deuteronomy who—more or less *en passant*—argues in this direction, is M. Noth, who claims that the use of אלהים instead of

---

[139] When Fishbane first launched the idea of a relationship between the two texts, he simply claims that "[…] Deut 4:16b–19a incorporates a polemical use of this sequence [= Gen 1:1–2:4a]"; cf. "Varia Deuteronomica", *Zeitschrift für die alttestamentliche Wissenschaft* 84 (1972) 349. In his *Biblical Interpretation in Ancient Israel* (1985) 321–322, the method of this "use" is identified as "aggadic exegesis".

[140] M. Fishbane, *Biblical Interpretation in Ancient Israel* (1985) 321.

[141] It should here be noticed that an early exponent of the interpretation history of vv. 16b–18 points in the same direction: cf. the Septuagint "correction" of the reduced כל־רמש באדמה of v. 18a, παντὸς ἑρπετοῦ ὃ ἕρπει ἐπὶ τῆς γῆς, which echoes the πάντων τῶν ἑρπετῶν τῶν ἑρπόντων ἐπὶ τῆς γῆς of Gen 1:26.

[142] It should be acknowledged that Knapp is aware of some of these examples, cf. D. Knapp, *Deuteronomium 4* (1987) 82 and 99; however, they play no role in his analysis.

יהוה in vv. 32 and 34, reflects the terminology of Gen 1.[143] More recently, actually at the time Knapp was accomplishing his investigation, A. Rofé surveyed the relevant material, and he lists as Priestly expressions some of the ones mentioned by Knapp, but also others: such as the *hiphil* ילד and the *niphal* ישׁ II in v. 25, and further the ברא אלהים in v. 32.[144] As for the two former terms, they are generally taken as belonging to the Priestly vocabulary.[145] And as for the latter expression, the ברא אלהים in v. 32, which textually is immediately followed by the expression the אדם על־הארץ, one is certainly reminded of a typical Priestly text as Gen 1. This is, in fact, the only Old Testament reference, besides Gen 1:27 and its close associate 5:1— that lets the verb ברא occur with אלהים as subject and אדם as object.

Against this background I find it is reasonable to argue that Deut 4 can be read as a text that deliberately refers to the creation poem in Gen 1 in its elaboration of the Second commandment. From the perspective of inner-biblical interpretation, I will conclude that the several examples of typical Priestly terminology function as markers, inviting the passages in Deut 4 in which this Priestly terminology occurs to be read together the Priestly texts to which they allude. And as far as vv. 16b–18 are concerned, this means that this passage ought to be read together with Gen 1, and then in particular Gen 1:26 f. The result is then that a distinct rhetorical nexus between the themes of creation and idolatry is established, according to Fishbane, in order to express that "[...] idolatry is sin against the creator and his transcendence".[146] And C.J. Labuschagne goes even one step further, as he explicitly states that Deut 4 turns around the order of the creation that is described in Gen 1:26–27: instead of man being made in the likeness of God, vv. 16b–18 portray a God that is made in the likeness of man.[147]

---

143 Cf. M. Noth, *Überlieferungsgeschichtliche Studien. Erster Teil* (1963 [1943]) 38, note 1.

144 A. Rofé, "The monotheistic argumentation in Deuteronomy iv 32–40: Contents, composition and text", *Vetus Testamentum* 35 (1985) 434–445; esp. p. 442.

145 *Niph.* the ישׁ II has only three occurrences, the one here in Deut 4:25, and then Lev 13:11 (P) and 26:10 (H); to P and *hiph.* the ילד, cf. J. Schreiner, "ילד", *Theologisches Wörterbuch zum Alten Testament* 3 (1982) 636 f.

146 See M. Fishbane, *Biblical Interpretation in Ancient Israel* (1985) 321-22.

147 See C.J. Labuschagne, *Deuteronomium 1A* (1987) 262-266, and especially p. 266: "Dit gevaar is niet denkbeeldig, met name als men bedenkt dat

The אשר-scheme

Let us then go to the אשר-scheme, and the relationship between the 3x
אשר-sentences in our passage and the corresponding three sentences in
the Decalogue version of the Second commandment, Deut 5:8 (= Exod
20:4).

Deut 5:8 (C)	Deut 4:17–18 (A)
אשר בשמים	כל־ בהמה אשר בארץ
ואשר בארץ	כל־ צפור כנף אשר תעוף בשמים
	כל־ רמש באדמה
ואשר במים מתחת לארץ	כל־ דגה אשר במים מתחת לארץ

The correspondence between the two texts is acknowledged by
many commentators. Still, a closer comparison of the two texts will
demonstrate that there are also some terminological and structural
differences. Let us therefore look at the relationship between the two
texts from two perspectives: (i) their terminological and structural
relationship, and (ii) their chronological relationship.

(i) Beginning with their terminological and structural relationship, I
would like to point out two areas of clear correspondence. First, from a
terminological point of view, it should be noticed that the third אשר-
sentence in our passage, ואשר במים מתחת לארץ, is identical with the third
אשר-sentence of both Decalogue versions of the Second commandment
(cf. Deut 5:8, Exod 20:4). These are the only three examples in the Old
Testament of this particular sentence, and this fact confirms the close
relationship between the texts. Secondly, from a structural point of view,
it should be noticed that the tripartite pattern reflected in both texts is
quite seldomly found in the Old Testament.[148] Generally speaking, the
Old Testament prefers a dual pattern of "heaven and earth" (cf. for
example v. 39 here in Deut 4), rather than a tripartite pattern of "heaven,
earth, and (whatever is) under the earth". Nevertheless, it is possible to

---

Israël geloofde dat de mens naar het beeld en in de gelijkenis van God
geschapen is. Man kan daarom gemakkelijk in de verleiding komen het
omgekeerde te gaan geloven, namelijk dat God gerepresenteerd kan worden
door een afbeelding van een menselijk wezen."

[148] It is often claimed that the tripartite pattern reflects Babylonian concepts of
the universe; cf. e.g. M. Dietrich & O. Loretz, *'Jahwe und seine Aschera'*
(1992) 37–38.

find tripartite patterns elsewhere in the Old Testament. A large scale parallel is found in Gen 1 and a small scale parallel can be found in Ps 115:15–17. As for the question of origin, the first of these point in the direction of the Priestly literary tradition,[149] whereas the second is related to the Priestly as well as the Deuteronomistic literary traditions.[150]

However, in addition to these two areas of close connection, I see two areas of difference. First, the successive order of the two tripartite systems: the Decalogue version (Deut 5:8) has (a) בשמים and (b) בארץ, whereas the allusion here in vv. 17–18 has (a) בארץ and (b) בשמים, and then both have (c) במים מתחת לארץ. One could perhaps say that the Decalogue version is the most logical one. Starting from above the series is arranged as (a) heaven, (b) earth, and (c) under the earth, whereas the allusion here in v. 17 more surprisingly arranges its series as (a) earth, (b) heaven, and (c) under the earth. Secondly, v. 18a raises some special problems. Compared with the other lines of vv. 16b–18, it lacks both a noun after כל־, and the relative pronoun אשר before באדמה. And further, this line has no counterpart in the Decalogue version of the commandment. A comparison of the two texts therefore demands a particular explanation of v. 18a.[151]

(ii) The obvious question is whether the terminological and structural relationship between the two texts can throw some light on their chronological relationship. The chronological relationship has traditionally been understood in the way that the Decalogue version is

---

[149] Cf. e.g. E. Nielsen, *Deuteronomium* (1995) 77, who argues the Second commandment (Deut 5:8b) reflects the same tripartite division of the universe as that of the Priestly creation account.

[150] The setting of Ps 115 is difficult to ascertain; still, several scholars relate it to a Priestly context, cf. H.-J. Kraus, *Psalmen 60–150* (1978[5]) 961–962. It should, however, be noticed that the polemic against idolatry earlier in Ps 115, especially in vv. 4–8, reflect a concept and a terminology one elsewhere encounters in Deuteronomistic literature, cf. Deut 4:28, 28:36.64, 27:15, 29:16, 31:29; see also M. Weinfeld, *Deuteronomy and the Deuteronomic School* (1972) 324 and 367.

[151] We are not the first to see these problems: the ancient *versiones* as well as more modern textual critics have made various attempts at harmonizing these gaps in the text, but with little success For a presentation of how the ancient *versiones* (*in casu* Targum Jonathan and the Septuagint) solve the problems, cf. above. With regard to literary critical attempts at solving the problems, cf. e.g. E. Nielsen, *Deuteronomium* (1995) 58, who argues: "Vielleicht ist ein רמש אשר durch Haplographie ausgefallen, vgl. LXX."

the source text upon which Deut 4:16b–18 depends and comments.[152] Since Deut 4 is acknowledged by most scholars as a very late text, this chronological relationship is in most cases simply taken for granted, without any further discussion of the matter.[153] However, as literary critics for quite some time now have argued that the tripartite section of the Second commandment is an addition,[154] it is not strange that the suggestion eventually has come up that it is the author of Deut 4:16b–18—with its 3x אשר-sentences—who is the one that is also responsible for the addition of the 3x אשר-sentences in (both versions of) the Second commandment. This suggestion is especially articulated by C. Dohmen. A post-exilic Pentateuch editor, according to Dohmen, introduced the 3x אשר-sentences in both versions of the Decalogue as an attempt at strengthening the Second commandment vis-à-vis the First, and the theological rationale for this was given by the same author in Deut 4:16b–18.[155]

I find Dohmen's suggestion quite speculative, and it actually creates more problems than it solves. I will instead, for three reasons, argue that the traditional understanding of the Decalogue version as the source text—upon which the passage here in vv. 17–18 depends and comments—is better. First, the successive order of the two tripartite systems. I find it difficult to see why the same author should give the theological rationale of the 3x אשר-sentences here in vv. 17–18, and then chose another successive order when he is to transfer this rationale into

---

[152] For an early example that explicitly argues in this direction, cf. A. Dillmann, *Die Bücher Numeri, Deuteronomium und Josua* (1886) 255–256, who in his analysis of Deut 4 argues: "Die beiden V. 17 f. mit ihrer Dreitheilung der Welt klingen wie eine Auslegung des Zehnworts Ex 20:4 (woher auch אשר במים מתחת לארץ wörtlich genommen ist)."

[153] Some examples from recent scholarship could be F.-L. Hossfeld, *Der Dekalog* (1982) 284; M. Weinfeld, *Deuteronomy 1–11* (1991) 205–206; and D.L. Christensen, *Deuteronomy 1–11* (1991) 86.

[154] An innovative role was here played by W. Zimmerli, "Das zweite Gebot", *Gottes Offenbarung* ([1950] 1963) 235; for a more recent literary critic following Zimmerli, cf. E. Nielsen, *Deuteronomium* (1993) 77

[155] Cf. C. Dohmen, *Das Bilderverbot* (1987) 223–229. For a survey of his literary critical reconstruction of the genesis of the Second commandment, cf. pp. 229–230. Dohmen says (cf. p. 201, note 405) that the literary critical analysis here is worked out in close collaboration with D. Knapp; cf. also D. Knapp, *Deuteronomium 4* (1987) 88–91.

the Decalogue version of the Second commanment. Rather, I find it more probable that the different successive order reflects the opposite: that the author of vv. 17–18 related the already existing 3x אשר-scheme of the Decalogue version of the Second commandment to another existing scheme, the תבנית-scheme, with its list of various creatures. As we saw above, the successive order of these lists of various creatures differs somewhat. Still, none of them starts with "birds". One can therefore assume that it could have been experienced as somewhat odd to start the אשר-scheme of v. 17 with "heaven". Against this background, and contrary to Dohmen, I find it probable that the different successive order between the two texts reflects a chronological relationship where vv. 17–18 makes use of an already existing אשר-scheme, and lets this scheme be adjusted to another existing scheme, the list of creatures reflected in the תבנית-scheme.[156]

Secondly, I would say that the particular problems of v. 18a—that it, seen within the structure of vv. 16b–18, lacks both a noun and the relative pronoun, and that it has no counterpart in the Decalogue version of the Second commandment—is also best understood in the same way. As for the structure of vv. 16b–18, Dohmen has no answer to why the author would let v. 18a stick out. And as for the relationship to the Decalogue version of the commandment, I find it difficult to see why the same author, according to Dohmen, in vv. 16b–18, would create a pattern of five (the תבנית-scheme) parts, where v. 18a sticks out like a sore thumb, and then would use only three of these when the whole thing was to be transferred into the Decalogue version of the commandment. Rather, I find it more probable that these problems, too, reflect an adjustment of the אשר-scheme to the תבנית-scheme. In other words, the author of vv. 16b–18 had at his disposal a fivefold list (the תבנית-scheme) which included two different groups related to "earth"/"ground" (beast and creep), and when this was to be combined with a tripartite list (the אשר-scheme) of the Second commandment, the result was the incompleteness of v. 18a.

And thirdly, also the well known logical difficulties of the אשר-sentences of the Decalogue versions of the Second commandment point in the same direction. Both versions of the Decalogue let the relative

---

[156] G. Braulik, *Die Mittel deuteronomischer Rhetorik* (1978) 43, does not attempt at explaining the difference between the two texts, but he notices that the sound parallels between the endings of vv. 17a+b (בשמים + בארץ) and 18b (במים ... בארץ) may have some rhetorical effect.

clauses modify the תמונה. This, however, creates a rather odd meaning; it is, for example, difficult to imagine how a תמונה, "that is in heaven above", at the same time can be made by humans. Logically, one would instead have expected the relative clauses to modify the כל, that is "the form of anything (כל) that is in heaven above". So is actually the case in the syntactically easier allusion to the Second commandment here in Deut 4:16b–18. Here, the inverted כל־תמונת focuses on "the form of *any* figure", and it also relates the 3x אשר-sentences to more obvious counterparts than the commandment does; the likeness of *any* beast that is on the earth, the likeness of *any* winged bird that flies in the air, and the likeness of *any* fish that is in the water under the earth. Earlier interpreters therefore suggested that the כל־תמונה of the commandment should be emended to תמונת כל־, in accordance with Deut 4:16. This suggestion has, however, no support in the Hebrew manuscripts, and is now generally abandoned.[157]

The syntactic relationship between the כל־תמונה of Second commandment and the following 3x אשר sentences remains a crux. Nevertheless, as far as the relationship between the Decalogue version of the Second commandment and our passage here in Deut 4:16b–18 is concerned, the chronology is quite clear.[158] On the one hand, it is difficult to understand why the author responsible for the syntactically clear Deut 4:16–18 should add a problematic כל־תמונה to the already existing syntactic difficulties of the Second commandment. On the other hand, however, it is quite easy to imagine how a chronologically later author of Deut 4:16–18, in a text alluding to the Second commandment, would want to clarify some of these syntactic difficulties. I would therefore argue that the actual verses here in Deut 4 are best understood as a commentary intended to emphasize this particular interpretation of the Second commandment: cultic images, in whatever form and of whatever god, are to be avoided!

In a sum, it seems to me that the author of vv. 16b–18 makes use of an existing scheme, the 3x אשר-scheme of the Second commandment.

---

157   Cf. e.g. the suggestion in *Biblia Hebraica Kittel* app. Exod 20:4; this suggestion is not repeated by *Biblia Hebraica Stuttgartensia*. For a criticism, cf. W. Zimmerli, "Das Zweite Gebot", *Gottes Offenbarung* ([1950] 1963) 235, n. 3.

158   Cf. E. Otto, *Das Deuteronomium im Pentateuch und Hexateuch* (2000) 171; cf. also *idem*, "Deuteronomium 4", T. Veijola (ed.), *Das Deuteronomium und seine Querbeziehungen* (1996) 219–220.

When the 3x אשר-scheme is combined with the 5x תבנית-scheme, some structural problems are bound to occur. But the author eventually decided to leave them there, and let the verses have some surprising gaps. As such the empty spaces of v. 18a reflects the author's respect for the dignified text he is alluding to.

Interpretive accent

What is then the interpretive accent of vv. 16b–18's allusions to the Second commandment? An answer to this question must allow the text to communicate on two levels. On its surface level the text communicates a literal and concrete interpretation of the commandment, warning against any making of cultic images. As we have seen above, the previous passage developed the prohibition against images of Yahweh to include images of non-yahwistic deities as well. This is implicitly supported by the present passage's listing of a great variety of anthropomorphic and theriomorphic images. Although it is possible to argue that some of these could be related to worship of Yahweh, the list as a whole gives clear associations of non-yahwistic religion.

It has not been important in my discussion to explore the religio-historical context and exegetical implications of this side of the text. However, let me here, in order to prevent the impression that I do not see this side, emphasize that the text has indeed a literal and concrete meaning. Historical critical scholars who have related this passage to religio-historical phenomena in ancient Israel as well as in the Ancient Near East are, of course, not mistaken. Textual and iconographic material from these regions certainly give evidence that the text describes phenomena one would encounter in real cultic life. As such the literal meaning of the text, a warning against any making of cultic images in the form of not only human beings, but also beasts and birds, creep and fish, certainly makes sense and deserves the attention it traditionally has received from its commentators.

However, the discussion earlier in this chapter should have demonstrated that the text also communicates at a deeper level. The schematic structure serves not only to focus on the variety of imaginable images, but also to expose how the passage is made up of two different schemes, one alluding to the Second commandment, the other alluding the creation poem in Gen 1, and in particular to the creation of man in Gen 1:26 f. The interpretive accent of the passage, therefore, is an explicit linking of the commandment and the concept of God as creator and man as God's creation. Gen 1:26 lets the very fact that man is created in the image of God be explicitly linked to man's duties vis-à-vis the rest of the creation: "[...] in our image according to our likeness, that they may rule the fish of the sea, etc." V. 28 links the two by two sets of parallel structures: first two parallel sentences: "And God blessed them, and God said to them", and then a series of five imperatives: "be fruitful, and multiply and fill the earth and subdue it and rule the fish of the sea, etc."

When our passage makes parallel allusions to the Second commandment and to the poem of the creation of man, the interpretive accent is therefore that the making of images reflects a destruction of the triangular relationship between God, humankind and the rest of the creation. Humanity's relationship to God is destroyed. The one made in the likeness of God, instead makes images in human likeness, thereby worshipping himself. But also humanity's relationship to the rest of the creation is destroyed. Instead of fulfilling his obligation to rule over the birds, animals and fish on God's behalf, the human instead makes images of these creatures, and worships them as gods.

• CHAPTER FIVE •

BOW DOWN TO THEM
AND WORSHIP THEM

ANALYSIS OF VV. 19-20

Turning from vv. 16b–18 to vv. 19–20, we come to a passage that is different in several respects. With regard to structure, the organizing is less strict than in vv. 16b–18, and with regard to content, the focus on images is replaced by a focus on astral deities.

> [19] *And so that you do not lift up your eyes to heaven and see the sun and the moon and the stars, all the host of heaven, so that you are drawn away and bow down to them and serve them, things which Yahweh your God has allotted to all the peoples under the whole heaven.* [20] *But Yahweh has taken you, and brought you out of the iron furnace, out of Egypt, to be a people of his own possession, as at this day.*

Chapter 1 noticed two sets of terminological markers in this passage, indicating an allusion to the Second commandment here too:

תעבדם	ולא	להם	תשתחוה	לא־	C 5:9a
ועבדתם		להם	והשתחוית ...	ופן	A 4:19

After the initial prohibition against making images, the Second commandment goes on saying that these images are not to be worshipped. The commandment uses the verb pair עבד/חוה, together with the pronominal suffixes ם-/להם, to express this, and the same verb pair, in the same order and with the same pronominal suffixes, occur in the present passage, vv. 19–20. However, the mere occurrence of this verb pair, even together with the corresponding pronominal suffixes, is not enough to legitimize this passage as an allusion to the Second commandment, as the verb pair is widely attested in Deuteronomistic literature, also together with these and similar pronominal suffixes. When I, nevertheless, acknowledge this passage as an allusion to the Decalogue version of the Second commandment, it is mainly because it fits into the general structure of vv. 9–31 as a successive interpretation of the Second commandment. Against this background I would actually say that if this verb pair had not been here, one would have asked if it somehow had fallen out.

Now, the verb pair and the two pronominal suffixes belong to a rather complex structure in the Decalogue versions of the Second commandment; one problem is that the verb pair elsewhere in the Deuteronomistic literature only refers to worship of gods, and not of images, another that the plural pronominal suffixes come as a surprise after the singular פסל. These two problems will have to be discussed before we turn to the allusion here in vv. 19–20. The following analysis will therefore concentrate on three areas: (1) the function of the verb pair and pronominal suffixes in the Decalogue versions of the Second commandment, (2) their contextual function here in Deut 4, and (3) the interpretive accent of the allusion.

The function of the verb pair and pronominal suffixes in the Second commandment

As just pointed out, the verb pair עבד/חוה and the two pronominal suffixes ם-/להם belong to a rather complex structure in the Decalogue versions of the Second commandment, Deut 5:8–10, Exod 20:4–6.

One problem is that the verb pair elsewhere in the Deuteronomistic literature only refers to worship of gods, and not of images.[159] Each of

---

[159] Cf. Deut 5:9, 8:19, 11:16, 17:3, 29:25 [ET 26], 30:17, Josh 23:16, Judg 2:19, 1 Kings 9:6.9, 2 Kings 17:35, Jer 13:10, 16:11, 22:9, 25:6.

the two verbs may be used with images as grammatical objects;[160] however, the point here is not each of the two verbs on an individual base, but the two as a pair. And this pair clearly constitutes a fixed expression, which is never used with images. The other problem is the plural pronominal suffixes ‏להם/ם‎-. In the Decalogue version of the Second commandment the two come as a logical surprise. After the singular noun ‏פסל‎ one would have expected that also the suffixes referring to this noun were in singular. These two problems of the Second commandment are closely interrelated, and they have received quite a deal of interest from historical-critical scholarship.

An innovative contribution in this respect was that of W. Zimmerli, half a century ago.[161] Zimmerli emphasized, first, that the verb pair ‏עבד/חוה‎ in Deuteronomistic literature only takes gods—and not idols—as grammatical objects, and, secondly, that there are no grammatical objects in the beginning of the Second commandment that correspond with the plural suffixes ‏להם/ם‎- later on.

First commandment	‏אלהים אחרים‎	pl.
Second commandment	‏פסל וכל־תמונה‎	sg.
	‏לא־תשתחוה להם ולא תעבדם‎	pl.

The application of the Second commandment, with its plural "bow down to them and serve them", is then, according to Zimmerli, a later addition to the original short form of the commandment, a short form parallel to the form of the First commandment. The theological motivation of this addition, Zimmerli argued, is to place the Second commandment in the shadow of the First, by building a bridge from the plural of the application, over the singular of the Second commandment, and back to the plural "other gods" of the First commandment.[162] This would explain the syntactic problem of the singular "image" vs the plural "them", and it

---

[160] The verbs ‏עבד‎ is used only 3x with ‏פסל‎ or ‏פסלים‎ (Ps 97:7, 2 Kings 17:41, 2 Chr 33:22), whereas ‏חוה‎ is used 10x (Exod 32:4, Lev 26:1, Isa 2:8.20, 44:15.17, 46:6, Jer 1:16, Micah 5:12, Ps 106:19); cf. the discussion in F.-L. Hossfeldt, *Der Dekalog* (1982) 24–26.

[161] Cf. W. Zimmerli, "Das Zweite Gebot", *Gottes Offenbarung* ([1950] 1963) 234–248.

[162] Cf. *ibid.*, 241–242.

would also explain the peculiar use of the verb pair עבד/חוה.[163] Zimmerli was thereby able to come up with an explanation which gives reasonable answers to the two major problems in the text, and his views were soon to be accepted in wide scholarly circles.[164]

A couple of decades ago, however, F.-L. Hossfeld pointed out that Zimmerli's interpretation only fits the asyndetic form of the Deuteronomy version of the Second commandment, whereas the syndetic form of the Exodus version actually has two grammatical objects: a *waw* is placed in between פסל and כל־תמונה, and thereby the text reads "an image *and* any form".[165] Thus, according to Hossfeld, whereas the Deuteronomy version of the Decalogue links the prohibition against images (Second commandment) closely to the prohibition against other gods (First commandment), the Exodus version gives it a more independent role:[166]

---

[163] Based on this observation, Zimmerli's conclusion is utterly clear: "Die Verbindung von [Exod 20:]5a [= Deut 5:9a] zum Bildgebot v. 4 [= Deut 5:8] is damit zerrissen"; cf. *ibid.*, 238.

[164] A few examples to illustrate this could be H. Graf Reventlow, *Gebot und Predigt im Dekalog* (1962) 29–44; G. von Rad, *Das fünfte Buch Mose* (1964) 41; A.D.H. Mayes, *Deuteronomy* (1979) 167; C.J. Labuschagne, *Deuteronomium 1B* (1987) 34–35; for further terminological analysis, cf. J.P. Floss, *Jahwe dienen – Göttern dienen* (1975) 164–180. For a survey of the subsequent discussion, cf. F.-L. Hossfeld, *Der Dekalog* (1982) 21–24, and also C. Dohmen, *Das Bilderverbot* (1987) 213–216.

[165] Also the ancient interpreters and translators seem to have struggled with the problem of the two versions of the Second commandment, and there is a strong tradition of harmonizing the two; however, always at the cost of the Deuteronomy version, as a number of Hebrew manuscripts as well as several classical translations render both in the syndetic form of Exod 20:4 (cf. app. in *Biblia Hebraica Stuttgartensia* to Deut 5:8), whereas none render both in the asyndetic form of Deut 5:8. In modern scholarship most interpreters understand the difference between the two versions as reflecting a theological development of the commandment; however, the harmonizing position is still attested, cf. D.L. Christensen, *Deuteronomy 1–11* (1991) 109–110, who explicitly argues that those witnesses going against the MT of Deut 5:8 should be followed.

[166] Cf. F.-L. Hossfeld, *Der Dekalog* (1982) 24.

Exod 20					Deut 5
אלהים אחרים	v. 3	pl.	pl.	v. 7	אלהים אחרים
פסל ו־כל־תמונה	v. 4	pl.	sg.	v. 8	פסל כל־תמונה
תשתחוה להם ולא תעבדם	v. 5	pl.	pl.	v. 9	תשתחוה להם ולא תעבדם

Hossfeld further argues that this independent role of the Exodus version, where the "bowing down to them and serving them" applies to the plural "images" of the Second commandment rather than to the "other gods" of the First, is younger than the less independent role of the Second commandment in the Deuteronomy version, and that it reflects a post-exilic development that is closely related to the polemic against images in Second Isaiah.[167]

A few recent scholars follow the suggestions of Zimmerli and Hossfeld. A major example here is C. Dohmen, who in his monograph on the textual and theological development of the Second commandment accepts the basic premises of Zimmerli, and who also follows the major arguments of Hossfeld. Dohmen agrees with Hossfeld with regard to the difference between the Deuteronomy and Exodus versions of the Second commandment, and he emphasizes even stronger than Hossfeld that the Deuteronomy version makes it an "Unter- oder Spezialfall" of the First commandment, whereas the Exodus version makes it the major commandment of the Decalogue.[168]

---

[167] Cf. *ibid.*, 26.

[168] Compared to Hossfeld, Dohmen actually takes several steps further (though, Hossfeld later follows Dohmen, cf. his "Zum synoptischen Vergleich der Dekalogfassungen", F.-L. Hossfeld (ed.), *Vom Sinai zum Horeb* (1989) 84–88), as he quite optimistically claims to be able to work out the four major stages of the textual and theological development of the Second commandment; cf. C. Dohmen, *Das Bilderverbot* (1987) 229–230: (i) In an early deuteronomic version of the Decalogue, the Second commandment consisted of the short prohibitive only (לא־תעשה־לך פסל). Structurally it then functioned as a parallel to the similar prohibitive of the First commandment. (ii) An exilic editor then added the "bow down to them and serve them", with its plural suffixes to the Second commandment, as a response to the situation of the Babylonian exile, where "other gods" were experienced mainly as "images". Thereby a close relationship was established between the First and Second commandments, and the Second commandment was made an "Unter- oder Spezialfall" of the First. (iii) The post-exilic author of Deut 4:15–16a*.19–28, who was the first to relate the

But there are also scholars who find that this focus on the plural suffixes ‏ם/להם‎- and the copulative *waw* becomes somewhat subtle. One example is A. Graupner, who argues that Hossfeldt and Dohmen make too much out of the single *waw*.[169] Another is M. Weinfeld, who rejects the idea that the difference between the asyndetic Deuteronomy form and the syndetic Exodus form of the commandment reflects any attempt at strengthening its independence, and, as for the objects of the verb pair, argues that "[...] there is no justification for the distinction between the *gods* and their representatives, the idols. Both the Exodus version and the Deuteronomic version, then, when speaking about *bowing down and serving*, refer to 'other gods' which is 'images'".[170]

In response to this, I would say that Zimmerli's initial observation with regard to the Old Testament use of the verb pair ‏עבד/חוה‎ should be accepted: it is established as a fact that the verb pair refers to worship of gods only, and not of images. I also find that Hossfeld and Dohmen basically are right when they emphasize the theological difference between the two versions of the Second commandment. Now, one can of course, with Graupner and Weinfeld, argue that one thereby faces the danger of reading too much into what certainly is a rather minor

---

mode of the Horeb theophany ("you did not see ‏כל־תמונה‎", v. 15) to the prohibition against making images ("so that you do not make for yourselves an image ‏כל־ תמונת‎", v. 16a), added the central expression of this relationship, ‏כל־תמונה‎, as an apposition to the ‏פסל‎ of the Second commandment. This, however, did not affect the dependence of the Second commandment upon the First. (iv) And then finally, at an even later stage, one of the Pentateuch editors placed a *waw* between ‏פסל‎ and ‏כל־תמונה‎ in the Exodus version of the Second commandment (The Deuteronomy version was left unchanged due to the dignity of this tradition). Thereby, in the Exodus version, the plural suffixes in "bow down to them and serve them" became related to a plural reference within the Second commandment itself ("an image and any form"), and the Second commandment regained some of its former independence of the First commandment.

[169] Cf. A. Graupner, "Zum Verhältnis der beiden Dekalogfassungen Ex 20 und Dtn 5", *Zeitschrift für die alttestamentliche Wissenschaft* 99 (1987) 308–329, esp. pp. 311–315; cf. also W.H. Schmidt & al., *Die Zehn Gebote* (1993) 65–68. Hossfeld then responds to Graupner in "Zum synoptischen Vergleich der Dekalogfassungen", F.-L. Hossfeld (ed.), *Vom Sinai zum Horeb* (1989) 873–117.

[170] See M. Weinfeld, *Deuteronomy 1–11* (1991) 291.

difference, a single *waw*! However, in the context of the two versions of the Decalogue, with their many examples of apparently subtle differences which nevertheless reflect theological significance,[171] I would be prepared to take the single *waw* as such an example. And my major witness here is, of course, Deut 4. As I have pointed out above, the introduction of the noun סמל in the interpretation of the Second commandment in Deut 4:15–16a directs the prohibition against making images towards including images of both Yahweh and non-yahwistic deities.[172] This is followed up in the subsequent passages, and it seems to be quite typical of Deut 4 to relate the Second commandment's prohibition against images closely to the First commandment's prohibition against other gods. It is here of less importance whether this connection historically is best explained as reflecting that (one of) the author(s) responsible for Deut 4 is also responsible for the Deuteronomy version of the Second commandment, as Dohmen puts it,[173] or, as I would be inclined to argue, that it rather reflects that the allusions to the Second commandment in Deut 4 represent an early stage of the interpretation history of the Deuteronomy version of this commandment. The major point is that the interpretive accent of Deut 4 corresponds with an interpretation of the Deuteronomy version of the Second commandment that acknowledges its close connection to the First commandment.

The contextual function of the allusion in vv. 19–20

Vv. 19–20 turn the attention away from the previous passages's focus on anthropomorphic and theriomorphic images, and to celestial bodies, that is astral deities. And they are here, all of them: the sun and the moon and the stars, all the host of heaven. Traditional literary critics who, for various reasons, want to see vv. 17–18 and 19–20 as belonging to different textual layers or blocks, tend to emphasize the new dimension of the material in v. 19.[174] And surely, there is a major difference

---

171 For examples, cf. F.-L. Hossfeld, *Der Dekalog* (1982) *passim*.

172 Cf. above, pp. 43–46.

173 Cf. C. Dohmen, *Das Bilderverbot* (1987) 229.

174 Cf. D. Knapp, *Deuteronomium 4* (1987) 71. Similar concerns are also expressed by B.B. Schmidt, "The aniconic tradition", D.V. Edelman (ed.), *The Triumph of Elohim* (1995) 83–88.

between the handmade images of the previous passage, and the astral deities that this passage treats. Still, there are several examples throughout the Deuteronomistic literature where the these different categories of entities are listed together:[175]

	Deut 4:16+19	Deut 17:3	2 Kgs 17:16	2 Kgs 21:3
Images	פסל תמונת כל־סמל		מסכה עגלים	
and poles			אשרה	אשרה
Gods		אלהים אחרים	בעל	בעל
and astral	שמש	שמש		
deities	ירך	ירח		
	כובבים			
	כל־צבא	כל־צבא	כל־צבא	כל־צבא
	השמים	השמים	השמים	השמים
Verbs	עבד/חוה	עבד/חוה	חוה/עבד	חוה/עבד

We notice here that the main expression used about the astral deities, "all the host of heaven", is an expression that may be listed together with more specified astral deities, such as "sun", "moon" or "stars", but that it may also be listed together with gods, such as Ba'al or the fixed expression "other gods", or images or poles. There is, accordingly, no reason to question the linking together of the images of vv. 16b–18 and the astral deities of vv. 19–20.

Let us then look at the function of the allusion to the Second commandment here in vv. 19–20, from two perspectives; first, its function within the passage, and then within the larger context of Deut 4.

Israel is here in vv. 19–20 warned against bowing down to and serving (verb pair: עבד/חוה) to these (pronominal suffixes: להם/ם-) astral deities. The logical development of the thought-lines of vv. 19–20 can be explained as a chiastic structure, where the outer parts (vv. 19a vs 20b),

---

[175]   Cf. M. Weinfeld, *Deuteronomy and the Deuteronomic School* (1972) 321. Both J.P. Floss, *Jahwe dienen – Göttern dienen* (1975) 164–180, and F. Hossfeld, *Der Dekalog* (1982) 24–26, distinguish (although not exactly in the same way) between one form (the older one) where the order is (i) עבד and (ii) חוה [Floss: שחה] and another form (the younger one) where the order is the opposite. In my opinion this distinction is too subtle; the material is not big enough for this kind of statistical conclusions.

and then also the inner parts (vv. 19b vs 20a), are allowed to contrast each other:

v. 19a	Israel: negative warning	Should not bow down to them and serve them
v. 19b	Yahweh: acts vs the peoples	Allots (חלק) the peoples to worship astral deities
v. 20a	Yahweh: acts vs Israel	Saves (לקח) Israel from the iron furnace
v. 20b	Israel: positive aim	Will become a people of Yahweh's inheritance

The passage introduces a triangular relationship between Yahweh, Israel and the other peoples. It starts with a negative warning to Israel: she should not expose herself to the cult of astral deities, by lifting her eyes to see the sun, moon and stars, and then bow down to them and serve them (v. 19a). However, the aim of this negative warning is a positive one: Yahweh wants Israel to remain his inheritance (v. 20b).[176] Then, the inner parts provide an exemplification of what it means to be Yahweh's inheritance. Israel has been saved by Yahweh from Egypt;[177] this means that she has an experience of a relationship to an acting and potent God (v. 20a), whereas the other peoples are allotted, by the same God, to non-acting and impotent astral deities (v. 19b, cf. also v. 28).

The relationship of the other peoples to Yahweh and to Israel in v. 19 is important. Still, in its history of interpretation there have been examples of scholars seeing too much in this verse of an Old Testament

---

[176] The strong character of v. 20 of describing an aim, is reflected in its use of prepositions: v. 20a describes "from where" with 2x successive examples of the preposition מן (מכור הברזל ממצרים), and v. 20b describes "to where" with 3x successive examples of the preposition ל (להיות לו לעם); cf. G. Braulik, *Die Mittel deuteronomischer Rhetorik* (1978) 45.

[177] To the metaphor כור הברזל ("iron furnace"), cf. D. Vieweger, "'... und führte euch heraus aus dem Eisenschmelzoven, aus Ägypten, ...'", P. Mommer & al. (eds.), *Gottes Recht als Lebensraum* (1993) 265–276; Vieweger argues that the metaphor has a double function: it refers to the tradition of the hard life in Egypt, but it also points to the exodus experience as what constituted Israel as a people.

legitimation of non-yahwistic religion.[178] It should be noticed that when
the text talks about the cultic life of other peoples, claiming that Yahweh
has allotted worship of astral deities to them,[179] the motivation is mainly
to point out the unique position of Yahweh. He is Lord of everything,
even of the other peoples and their gods, and his own people Israel is
expected to reflect this.[180] The reference to the exodus experience serves
to express this. Partly, this reference is part of an interpretive tendency
throughout Deut 4 of relating the Second commandment to major phases
in the history of Israel. Partly, however, the reference to the exodus
experience also serves a more particular role here in v. 20, as exodus
from Egypt is *the* central example in the Deuteronomistic literature that
Yahweh is stronger than other gods and peoples. A similar thought is
found also in the frame texts of this chapter. Vv. 6–8 and 32–34, each of
them in a series of rhetorical questions, express how the other peoples
will be amazed by watching a people living near its God, through decrees
and judgements, vv. 6–8, and a God living near its people, through
theophany and salvation, vv. 32–34.

In other words, the function of the references to the other peoples
and their relationship to the astral deities is to create a contrastive
background for an understanding of the particular relationship between
Yahweh and Israel. This is expressed through two sets of contrasting
terminology; a play on sound and a play on meaning. Yahweh acts vis-à-
vis the other peoples as well as vis-à-vis Israel: he allots (contrasting key
word: חלק) the other peoples to worship astral deities, whereas he acts to
save (contrasting key word: לקח) Israel.[181] Therefore, if Israel should

---

[178]   An old, but still illustrative example of this tendency is A. Dillmann, *Die
        Bücher Numeri, Deuteronomium und Joshua* (1886) 256, who argues that
        "[…] vielmehr besagt der Ausdruck, dass die Verehrung der Gestirne durch
        die Völker im Willen des weltregierenden Gottes begründet sei. Das, was
        factisch besteht, wird auf den Willen Gottes zurückgeführt."

[179]   An echo of the same thought appears in Deut 29:25 [ET 26], there,
        however, it has a more negative function about Israel: Israel went and
        worshipped other gods and bowed down to them, gods whom they had not
        known and whom Yahweh had not allotted (חלק) to them.

[180]   See e.g. D. Knapp, *Deuteronomium 4* (1987) 186 (note 399); H.D. Preuss,
        Verspottung fremder Religionen (1971) 241–242.

[181]   The word play on לקח/חלק is recognized by several interpreters; G.
        Braulik, *Die Mittel deuteronomischer Rhetorik* (1978) 45, as one would

ever engage in astral worship—and the verb pair עבד/חוה is used to express this—she will eventually become like "all the peoples (contrasting key word: עמים) under the whole heaven", rather than being what she is called by Yahweh to remain, like "today": "a people (contrasting key word: עם) of his inheritance".

Let us then proceed to the function of the allusion within the larger context of Deut 4. I wrote in the beginning of this chapter that if the verb pair עבד/חוה were missing within the successive interpretation of the Second commandment in vv. 9–31, one would have asked whether it somehow had fallen out. Such a judgement is of course impossible to prove, but I would still mean that the verb pair comes at the right place in this successive interpretation; it is, so to speak, expected. Within the larger context of Deut 4, the verb pair עבד/חוה serves to relate the discourse in vv. 19–20 on astral worship to the more general interpretation of the Second commandment. This is reflected through the פן...ופן-structure of vv. 16 and 19. We have seen above that the series of פן in Deut 4 partly has the function of binding together and partly of transforming the prohibitive לא of the Decalogue into the parenetic context of Deut 4.[182] In parallel with the opening verses of the Decalogue, although in opposite order, the פן...ופן-structure of vv. 16 and 19 then serves to link the two topics "images" and "astral deities".

	Deut 5: Decalogue		Deut 4: Interpretation	
4	Yahweh spoke to you out of the fire		15	Yahweh spoke to you out of the fire	
7	no other gods	לא	16–18	no images	פן
8–10	no image	לא	19–20	no astral deities	ופן

---

expect; but even D. Knapp, *Deuteronomium 4* (1987) 74, is able to argue that a word play "möglicherweise" is intended.

[182] The פן-structures in Deut 4 was discussed above, cf. pp. 38–40. To the rhetorical function of the term, see G. Braulik, *Die Mittel deuteronomischer Rhetorik* (1978) 117. The present פן...ופן-structure (vv. 16–19) presents a problem to interpreters who see different hands at work in these verses; they can either ignore the structural relationship between the two, cf. E. Nielsen, *Deuteronomium* (1995) 40–61; or they can let it be a sign that vv. 16 and 19 belong together; cf. D. Knapp, *Deuteronomium 4* (1987) 71, who is able to recognize the relationship between the 2x פן, as he takes vv. 15–16a* and 19–28 (without vv. 16b*–18) as belonging to the same block.

This linking does not mean that the text suddenly leaves its hitherto interpretation of the Second commandment and becomes an interpretation of the First. The context of v. 19's reference to astral deities is still located within the context of an interpretation of the Second commandment; the verb pair is still alluding to the Second commandment, and, if the reader for some reason should forget that it all is related to the commandment against making images (v. 16), the very centre of the commandment is soon to be repeated, even twice (vv. 23 and 25). Still, at the same time it is clear that a new entity actually is brought into the interpretation of the Second commandment, namely astral deities, and the פן...ופן-structure serves to link the warning against these deities to the warning against images of the preceding verses.

Interpretive accent

What is then the interpretive accent of vv. 19–20's allusion to the Second commandment? The relationship between the nouns פסל and תמונה attested in both versions of the Decalogue have been analyzed, with particular reference to their relationship to the verb pair עבד/חוה and the pronominal suffixes להם/ם-. It has been pointed out that the basic problem of the Decalogue versions is whether these markers refer to the "other gods" of the First commandment or the "image(s)" of the Second commandment. And it has been argued that the two Decalogue versions of the commandment reflect different understandings of the relationship between the First commandment's prohibition of other gods and the Second commandment's prohibition of images. Whereas the asyndetic Deuteronomy version tends to link the two commandments close to each other, the asyndetic Exodus version tends to emphasize a more independent role of the Second commandment.

As for the interpretation of the Second commandment offered here in vv. 19–20, one could probably say that it takes sides in this unclear situation, and supports the Deuteronomy version of the Decalogue. The two sets of terminological markers, the verb pair עבד/חוה and the pronominal suffixes להם/ם-, are here explicitly related to the astral deities of v. 19, and not to the images of vv. 16 ff. As such, the allusion reflects an interpretation that takes the Second commandment in one particular direction: its prohibition against making images is seen as just another side of the coin of the First commandment's prohibition against other gods. This interpretation is then linked to Israel's historical experience of being freed from Egypt. Through the exodus experience, Israel was made Yahweh's special possession, and her worship of Yahweh therefore must differ from other peoples' worship of their gods.

• CHAPTER SIX •

A JEALOUS GOD

ANALYSIS OF VV. 21-24

The next passage in the successive interpretation of the Second commandment starts with a narrative section referring to the tradition about Moses not being allowed into the promised land (vv. 21–22), and this then provides a background for a more paraenetic section (vv. 23–24).

> [21] *And Yahweh was angry with me because of you, and he swore that I should not cross the Jordan, and that I should not enter the good land which Yahweh your God is giving you as an inheritance.* [22] *For I must die in this land, I shall not cross the Jordan. But you will cross and take possession of that good land.* [23] *Be careful, so that you not forget the covenant of Yahweh your God which he made with you, and make for yourselves an image in the form of anything which Yahweh your God has forbidden you.* [24] *For Yahweh your God is a consuming fire, a jealous God.*

Chapter 1 noticed two sets of terminological markers in this passage, thereby indicating two allusions to the Second commandment; one to its opening line, ועשיתם לכם פסל תמונת כל, and another to its motivation, כי יהוה אלהיך ... אל קנא.

C 5:8aα.9bα	לא תעשה לך	פסל	כל־תמונה	כי אנכי יהוה	אל קנא
A 4:23b–24	ועשיתם לכם	פסל	תמונת כל	כי יהוה	אל קנא

Against this background, the following analysis of vv. 21–24 will concentrate on three areas: analyses of the contextual function of the first (1) and second (2) of these allusions, and (3) the interpretive accent of the allusions.

The contextual function of the allusion in v. 23

The first allusion to the Second commandment in this passage, v. 23's allusion to the opening line of the commandment, is one of three quite similar examples throughout the core vv. 9–31 of Deut 4.

4:16	ועשיתם	לכם	פסל	תמונת	כל־	סמל
4:23	ועשיתם	לכם	פסל	תמונת	כל	
4:25	ועשיתם		פסל	תמונת	כל	

The only major difference between the three cases are found in their respective conclusions, after their common expressions תמונת כל. On the one hand, v. 16 concludes the inverted allusion to the commandment's כל־תמונה by adding the term סמל, which, as we have seen previously, is part of a gradual opening towards including images of non-yahwistic deities in the interpretation of the Second commandment: "an image, the form of any figure".[183] On the other hand, vv. 23 and 25 let the final כל also be the conclusion of the allusion: "an image, the form of anything". After vv. 19–20's explicit reference to non-yahwistic deities the concern of v. 16's סמל can now be taken for granted.

Let us then take a closer look at the structure of v. 23.

v. 23a	השמרו לכם פן תשכחו את ברית יהוה אלהיכם אשר כרת עמכם
v. 23b	ועשיתם לכם פסל תמונת כל אשר צוך ...

The introductory phrase "Be careful, so that you not [...]", recalls a frequently attested pattern in Deut 4: a combination of *niphal* of שׁמר together with the negative telic particle פֶּן; cf. vv. 9.15.16.19.23. And, as

---

[183] Cf. above, pp. 43–46.

I have pointed out previously, the function of the פן in this context of allusions to the Second commandment is to transform the prohibitive form of the Decalogue version of the commandment into the present context of paraenetic exposition.[184] This introductory phrase then governs two structurally parallel sentences (vv. aβγ and b), each consisting of (i) a verb that expresses the idea of the negative telic particle, (ii) a phrase that describes the two contrasting entities, and (iii) a relative clause that motivates the preceding contrasting phrases. The parallelism between the two verbs (3. p. pl.) in (i) is quite obvious, and so is the parallelism between the two motivations (אשר + Yahweh vs "you") in (iii). Let me, however, comment on (ii), which relates the making of images to the forgetting of the ברית. Whereas the first passage in Deut 4's successive interpretation of the Second commandment, vv. 9–13, lets the ברית be identified as the Decalogue as a whole (v. 13), v. 23 can now, after the preceding focus on the Decalogue commandment against making images, let this particular commandment summarize what it means to forget the ברית. In other words, as a consequence of Deut 4's focus on the Second commandment, a violation against this commandment can here be understood as a violation against the Decalogue as such, and then even of Yahweh's ברית with Israel.

What is then the contextual function of v. 23's allusion to the Second commandment? The major perspective here, I will argue, is that it relates the allusion to major experiences from the history of Israel. Also in the previous passage, vv. 19–20, we saw that its allusions to the commandment were related to Israel's history, in that case to the exodus experience. The present passage continues this chronologically, relating its allusions to the next steps in this history; first the rebellion against Yahweh in the desert (vv. 21–22a), then the crossing of the river Jordan, and finally the subsequent occupation of the promised land (v. 22b).

The reference to the rebellion in the desert focuses on its consequences for Moses; he will not be allowed to enter the promised land.[185] Two other texts in the same literary tradition also refer to the rebellion, thereby providing some comparative material for the analysis of our text; the two are Deut 1:19–46 and Deut 3:23–29. First, a comparison of vv. 21–22 with these two texts shows that the central

---

[184] Cf. above, pp. 38–40.

[185] This is not a digression, as D. Knapp, *Deuteronomium 4* (1987) 75, puts it; rather, it is the major point of the passage.

motive is the same in all three texts: Yahweh gets angry with Moses
"because of you".[186] Secondly, however, it also shows that even though
the motive is the same, it is used differently in the three texts. The first
two use it quite similarly: the first tells a narrative about the people
making a rebellion against Yahweh, with the result that "not a man of
this generation will see the good land" (v. 35), and the second, also this
in the form of a narrative, tells how Moses questions Yahweh's decision
of not even letting him enter the land. But when it comes to the third text,
our vv. 21–22, the tradition about Moses not being allowed into the good
land is given a theological re-orientation. Let me make two remarks
about this.

First, vv. 21–22 portray Moses as playing a theologically more
significant role than what is the case in the two parallel texts. In Deut 1
the whole generation that participated in the rebellion is denied access to
the good land, and Moses together with them. But here in vv. 21–22 only
Moses is mentioned. And, Moses seems to be punished on behalf of the
people. This is expressed by two sets of contrasts; first, it is argued that
Yahweh is angry with Moses "because of you" (על־דבריכם), and then, in
the form of a chiasm,[187] it is argued that whereas Moses will not be
crossing (איני עבר) Jordan and come to the good land, Israel will cross
(ואתם עברים) Jordan and take possession of the good land. The Moses-
figure is important also elsewhere here in Deut 4, being portrayed as a
mediator of the word of Yahweh (see vv. 1.2.5.8.14.40). Still, in vv. 21–
22, the role of being a mediator has got a new dimension. Moses is not
only Yahweh's representative versus Israel, he is now also portrayed as
Israel's representative versus Yahweh, who is made responsible by
Yahweh for the sins of the people as a whole. The fact that Moses is
denied access to the promised land thereby exemplifies the consequences
that the people eventually will have to face if they continue to neglect
Yahweh's commandments, and as such the tradition about Moses

---

[186]   The "because of you" is expressed differently in the three texts: Deut 1:37
has בגללכם, 3:26 has למענכם, and 4:21 has על־דבריכם. Only the first text
(Deut 1:19–46) provides information about what lies in the "because of
you": a reference to the rebellion against Yahweh; the other two texts say
no more, it seems that it is taken for granted that the readers are now
acquainted with the information of the first chapter.

[187]   The chiasm is discussed by G. Braulik, *Die Mittel deuteronomischer
Rhetorik* (1978) 46.

referred to in vv. 21–22 prepares for the emphasizing of Yahweh as a jealous God in v. 24.

Secondly, the tradition about Moses not being allowed to enter the good land is here in vv. 21–22 linked to a warning against making images, vv. 23–24. The verb used to express Yahweh's anger, אָנַף, which is also used in the first of the three texts (Deut 1:37),[188] has strong connotations in Deuteronomistic literature to Yahweh's anger against "images" and "other gods".[189] It is used seven times within the Deuteronomistic tradition, and, except the two ones here, Deut 1:37 and 4:21, four of the remaining five occurrences are found in contexts of "images" and "other gods": Deut 9:8 and 20 relates it to the episode of the golden calf at Horeb, 1 Kings 11:9 relates it to the "other gods" of king Solomon's foreign wives (cf. vv. 8 and 10), and 2 Kings 17:18 relates it to the judgement over the Northern Kingdom, where the accusation of worship of "images" and "other gods" is at the very center. The fifth occurrence, 1 Kings 8:46, from Solomon's prayer of dedication, could also very well fit into this pattern, as it talks in very general terms about the possibility that the people might sin against Yahweh.

Against this background, I would argue that the verb אָנַף, which (a) is used by Deut 1:37 in the narrative about Israel's rebellion, legitimizing that the present generation, including Moses, is not to be allowed into the promised land, and (b) with its strong connotations in Deuteronomistic literature of Yahweh's anger against "images" and "other gods", probably is the key word that enabled the author of vv. 21–24 to link the tradition of Moses being punished on behalf of the people to the present context of interpretation of the Second commandment.

The contextual function of the allusion in v. 24

The series of terminological markers alluding to the Second commandment in v. 24 actually make up most of this short verse, only the expression אֵשׁ אֹכְלָה הוּא is not taken from the commandment:

---

[188] There are also other terminological examples showing that Deut 4:21–22 is closer to Deut 1:19–46 than to Deut 3:23–29; cf. especially the verb שָׁבַע, Deut 1:34 and 4:21.

[189] Cf. M. Weinfeld, *Deuteronomy and the Deuteronomic School* (1972) 346.

אל קנא	יהוה אלהיך	אנכי	כי	C	5:9
אל קנא אש אכלה הוא	יהוה אלהיך		כי	A	4:24

Let us look at the verse from two perspectives, first the general Old Testament usage of the main marker, the expression אל קנא, and then its contextual function.

The expression אל קנא, "a jealous God",[190] occurs only six times in the Old Testament; two of which are the Decalogue versions of the Second commandment, and a third is our text here in v. 24. The remaining three, Deut 6:15 and Exod 34:14 (2x), may then shed some light also on the ones related explicitly to the Second commandment. In Deut 6, where the context is a list of warnings to Israel before she goes into the promised land (vv. 10–25), Israel is first warned against following the אלהים אחרים of the peoples around (v. 14), and then this warning is motivated by a reference to Yahweh as an אל קנא (v. 15). In Exod 34, where the context is the narrative about the golden calf (Exod 32–33) and the subsequent renewal of the covenant (Exod 34), it is said that Aaron "made it [the gold] to a molten calf" (Exod 32:4a),[191] and then follows a quotation saying that "these are your gods, O Israel, that brought you up out of the land of Egypt" (32:4b). As part of the renewal of the covenant, Exod 34:13–17 tells Israel to destroy the pillars and Asheras of the other peoples, and not worship other gods or make images, because Yahweh, whose name is קנא, "Jealous", he is an אל קנא, a jealous God, v. 14. Seeing the material as a whole, it is clear that the two אל קנא-texts outside the Decalogue and Deut 4 make no clear distinction between Yahweh's jealousy vis-à-vis "other gods" or "images", that is vis-à-vis the First and Second commandments. Rather, it seems that the two texts refer to the first two commandments together.

Secondly, back in Deut 4, v. 24 lets the expression אל קנא act as an apposition to the sentence אש אכלה הוא: "Yahweh your God is a consuming fire, a jealous God." This sentence, which is added to and integrated into the commandment allusion, serves to relate the allusion to

---

[190]   For a general discussion of the Hebrew root קנא, cf. E. Reuter, "קנא", *Theologisches Wörterbuch zum Alten Testament* 7 (1993) 51–62; cf. especially cols. 58–60, where the Old Testament references to אל קנא are discussed.

[191]   The verb for "making" is here in Exod 32:4 the same as in the Second commandment, עשה; the corresponding text in Deut 9:16 is closer to the commandment, with עשה plus לכם.

אל קנא to the wider context of Deut 4, where the key word, אֵשׁ, "fire", occurs six times. The other five אֵשׁ-references use the key word to describe the mountain, Horeb, burning with fire (v. 11, cf. also Deut 5:23) or Yahweh speaking "out of the midst of the fire" (vv. 12.15.24.33.35, cf. also Deut 5:4.22.24.26), whereas it in v. 24 is given a more particular usage: Yahweh himself is an אֵשׁ אכלה. It is difficult to say what concepts of Yahweh are expressed in the description of him as "a consuming fire". According to Exod 24:17, the glory of Yahweh looked "like a consuming fire (כאֵשׁ אכלת)" on the top of the mountain, but the present text goes further in identifying Yahweh and the fire. A terminological parallel, which also emphasizes the dangerous connotations, is Deut 5:25: "a great fire (האֵשׁ הגדלה) will consume us (תאכלנו) if we hear the voice of Yahweh or God any longer".

However, the expression אֵשׁ אכלה is found one more time in the Old Testament: Deut 9:3, which belongs to a context that includes the Deuteronomy version of the narrative about the golden calf (Deut 9:1–10:11).[192] Like the Exod 32–34 version of this narrative (cf. above), also the Deut 9–10 version portrays the actual making of the calf with a terminology that alludes to the Second commandment, and both also let "fire" play a role in the destruction of the calf: it is put on the fire (Exod 32:20.24, Deut 9:21). Still, it is only in Deut 9–10 one can say that אֵשׁ really acts as a key word: Yahweh speaks out of the fire (Deut 9:10, 10:4) and the mountain is burning with fire (Deut 9:15). It is therefore not surprising that it is only in the Deut 9–10 version that Yahweh is portrayed as אֵשׁ אכלה.

Against this background I will argue that both the Exodus and Deuteronomy versions of the narrative about the golden calf contribute material to the interpretation of the Second commandment in our vv. 23–24. The Exod 32–34 version provides one of the key expressions, אל קנא, which makes it possible to relate the commandment to the golden calf narrative, whereas the Deut 9–10 version provides the other key expression, אֵשׁ אכלה, which makes it possible to relate the commandment to the overall background of Deut 4, the Horeb theophany.[193]

---

[192] Cf. above, pp. 88–89, where some other aspects of the terminological correspondence between Deut 4:21 and 9:8.20 are discussed.

[193] This would correspond with E. Otto, *Das Deuteronomium im Pentateuch und Hexateuch* (2000) 168, who argues that the focus of Deut 4 is not only the Horeb material of Deuteronomy, but also the Sinai material of Exodus.

Interpretive accent

What is then the interpretive accent of vv. 21–24's allusion to the Second commandment? In sum I would say that the passage confirms the tendency we have noticed also in the previous passages of linking the Second commandment's prohibition against images to the First commandment's prohibition against "other gods". This interpretive accent is expressed through two references to Israel's experiences with and understanding of Yahweh on her way from Egypt to the promised land; Moses being denied access to the land, and Yahweh as a consuming fire. Both are wrapped in a language that has connotations to Israel's sin against the Second commandment, and as such the function of both the references to Israel's experiences and the allusions to the Second commandment is to warn Israel against the making of images.

• CHAPTER SEVEN •

CHILDREN AND GRANDCHILDREN

ANALYSIS OF VV. 25-31

The final passage within the successive interpretation of the Second commandment in the core of Deut 4 is vv. 25–31, and here it is the future generations that are focused. What will their destiny be like, in the land on the other side of the river Jordan?

[25] *Should you, when you have begotten children and grandchildren, and have grown old in the land, act corruptly by making an image in the form of anything, and do what is evil in the eyes of Yahweh your God, to provoke him,* [26] *I call heaven and earth to witness against you today, that you will soon utterly perish from the land which you are crossing the Jordan to possess; you will not live long upon it, but will be utterly destroyed.* [27] *And Yahweh will scatter you among the peoples, and you will be left few in number among the nations where Yahweh will drive you.* [28] *And there you will serve gods of wood and stone, the work of man's hands, that neither see, nor hear, nor eat, nor smell.* [29] *But from there you will seek Yahweh your God, and you will find, if you search him with all your heart and with all your soul.* [30] *When you are in trouble, and all these things come upon you in the latter days, you will return to Yahweh your God and obey his voice.* [31] *For Yahweh your God is a merciful God; he will not fail you and not*

destroy you and not forget the covenant with your fathers, which he swore to them.

Chapter 1 noticed two sets of terminological markers in this passage, indicating two allusions to the Second commandment, one is the expression בנים ובני בנים in v. 25a, another is the phrase ועשיתם תמונת כל in v. 25b:

על־בנים	כל־תמונה פסל תעשה־לך לא־	C	5:8aα+9bβ
בנים ובני בנים		A	4:25aα
	פסל תמונת כל ועשיתם	A	4:25bα

The phrase ועשיתם תמונת כל in v. 25b is obviously an allusion to the Second commandment; it has been noticed several times already that it is the third in a series of three more or less similar allusions, cp. vv. 16 and 23. But is it correct to say that also the expression בנים ובני בנים in v. 25a is an allusion to the Second commandment? Is not a repetition of one single word—even though it is a thematic key word like בנים—too little to be recognized as an allusion? I admit that it is little. Nevertheless, I will argue that this expression in v. 25a alludes to the בנים of the commandment, and that it, like the following, clearer example in v. 25b, serves to relate the passage to which it belong to the successive interpretation of the commandment. I have four reasons for arguing this. First, because this understanding of the expression בנים ובני בנים fits into the general structure of vv. 9–31 as a successive interpretation of the Second commandment. Actually, without such an understanding of this expression, the successive interpretation of the commandment would end quite abruptly midways, with a reference to Yahweh as אל קנא, and without letting the positive concerns of the final sentence of the commandment being reflected. Secondly, because of the cumulative force of the preceding allusions; now, towards the end of the successive interpretation of the commandment, the need for explicit markers is less than in the beginning of the interpretation. Thirdly, because the noun בנים is an important key word in the latter half of the commandment. V. 25 does not repeat and elaborate just any accidental word; בנים is a key word that catces the very point of the second half of the commandment, the destiny of the future generations. And fourthly, because v. 25 explicitly links the expression בנים ובני בנים (v. 25a) to the more obvious allusion to the commandment, the phrase ועשיתם פסל תמונת כל (v. 25b).

The following analysis of vv. 25–31 will concentrate on three areas: (1) the second (for pragmatic reasons) and (2) first of these two allusions, and (3) the interpretive accent of the allusions.

The contextual function of the allusion in v. 25b

V. 25b contains the third and last example of Deut 4's triple allusions to the introductory words of the Second commandment, cp. vv. 16 and 23. As we have seen previously, v. 16 lets its marker תמונת כל be continued by the noun סמל, which enables the commandment against images of Yahweh also to include images of non-yahwistic deities. Vv. 23 and 25 lack the סמל; it has probably served its purpose in v. 16, and the two latter examples let the final כל also be the conclusion of the allusion: "an image, the form of anything".

Two aspects of the contextual function of the ועשׂיתם פסל תמונת כל here in v. 25 should be noticed. First, by help of the verb עשׂה, a parallelism is created between v. 25bα and 25bβ:

פסל תמונת כל	ועשׂיתם	והשחתם	v. 25bα
הרע בעיני יהוה־אלהיך להכעיסו	ועשׂיתם		v. 25bβ

The sentence which thereby is parallelled with the making of images—"do what is evil in the eyes of Yahweh your God, to provoke him"—has a motive and a terminology which Deuteronomistic literature generally uses against images and other gods. The motive, which normally uses some form of the verb עשׂה and then the fixed word combination הרע בעיני יהוה, is attested three more times in Deuteronomy: first, in 9:18, where it is used with reference to the making of the golden calf (cf. v. 16); further, in 17:2, where it is used with reference to worship of other gods, "or to the sun, the moon, or any of the host of heaven" (v. 3); and finally, in 31:29, where it is used without any direct reference to images or other gods, but where the term רע is closer identified as במעשׂה ידיכם, "by the work of your hands", which, in Deuteronomistic literature, is a typical reference to images or idols.[194]

---

[194] Cf. S.R. Driver, *A Critical and Exegetical Commentary on Deuteronomy* (1978³) 344, who argues that Deut 31:29 refers to a systematic engagement in idolatrous practices.

Secondly, the motive of v. 25bα is followed up in v. 28. The terminology of the commandment is here replaced by terms that seem to express a somewhat harsher mood: the central verb עשׂה is reflected in the expression מעשׂה ידי אדם, "fashioned by the hands of man", and these examples of handicrafts are then identified as gods that neither see, nor hear, nor eat, nor smell. The identification in v. 28 of the gods—some Hebrew manuscripts and classical translations have "other gods", just to make the point—as מעשׂה ידי אדם, is a typical example of Deuteronomistic terminology and concepts.[195] Here, it serves to continue and express explicitly a conceptual pattern I have pointed out several times of linking the First and Second commandment within Deut 4.

The thematic continuity which thereby is created from v. 25 to v. 28 is important, as it explicitly relates the breaking of the Second commandment to the exile. After v. 25's allusions to the commandment, v. 26 emphasizes Yahweh's response by two parallel cases of infinitive absolute: "you will utterly perish" (אבד תאבדון), and "you will utterly be destroyed" (השמד תשמדון), and v. 27 even lets Yahweh be the explicit, grammatical subject of the scattering of Israel among the nations. Still, this is a complex relationship. The exile is a result of Israel breaking the Second commandment, and the exile is also a context of continued breaking of the commandment; nevertheless, at the same time the exile is a context from which Israel will repent from her breaking the commandment, v. 29.

The contextual function of the allusion in v. 25a

Let us then turn to the first allusion to the Second commandment in this passage, the expression בנים ובני בנים in v. 25aα. As indicated above, I believe that this expression alludes to the key word בנים in the latter part

---

[195] M. Weinfeld, *Deuteronomy and the Deuteronomic School* (1972) 324, lists the following references to the concept of human-created gods: Deut 4:28, 27:15, 28:64, 31:29; and then also 1 Kings 16:7, 2 Kings 19:18, 22:17. For a discussion of how this typical Deuteronomistic terminology is also reflected in Hosea, cf. *ibid.*, 367; cf. Hos 13:2, 8:6, 14:4, 4:12. The concept that these man-made gods neither see nor hear, etc., has its closest parallels in Pss 115:5–7 and 135:16–17.

of the commandment; Deut 5:9b–10, Exod 20:5b–6.[196] I find that it catches the very point of this latter part's application of the commandment, the question about the destiny of the future generations in relation to the commandment, and that it as such serves, to link the present passage to the commandment, not only terminologically but also thematically. Two things should here be analyzed: the destiny of the future generations according to the passage vv. 25–31, and their destiny when this passage is taken as an interpretation of the Second commandment.

First, it is clear that the contextual function of the בנים ובני בנים is to introduce the exile. The logical structure of the following verses corresponds with major lines in Deuteronomistic historiography; the crossing of the Jordan, the occupation of the land, sin against (the Second commandment and) Yahweh, with the exile as the logical consequence, and then finally a return to Yahweh, provided you—that is the בנים ובני בנים—seek him "with all your heart and all your soul" (v. 29). Also the terminology that is used reflects typical Deuteronomistic terminology related to the exile; cf. e.g. פוץ (cf. Deut 28:64, 30:3), שאר (cf. Deut 28:62, 2 Kings 19:30), and צרר (cf. Deut 28:52).

It should here be noticed that v. 31 concludes the core text of Deut 4 by drawing some of its central thoughts together, and use them to make a profiled presentation of Yahweh versus Israel.[197] One example is when v. 31 says that Yahweh will "not destroy you (שחת) and not forget (שכח) the covenant with your fathers". This contrasts Israel, which "corrupts itself" (שחת, vv. 16 and 25) and "forgets" (שכח, v. 23) the same covenant, a covenant where the prohibition against making images is central.[198] The function of this juxtapositioning is to point out Yahweh as one that can be trusted. This means that even Israel, which herself is not to be trusted, should trust in Yahweh. Another example in the same direction occurs in v. 31, which says that Yahweh is an אל רחום, "merciful God". The expression אל רחום contrasts v. 24, where Yahweh quite contrary is presented as an אל קנא, "a jealous God", and an אש אכלה, "a consuming

---

[196] The difference between 5:9's polysyndetic על־בנים ועל־שלשים ועל־רבעים and Exod 20:5's asyndetic על־בנים על־שלשים ועל־רבעים is mostly taken as a stilistic variation; however, F.-M. Hossfeld, *Der Dekalog* (1982) 26–32, takes it as an older versus a younger way of counting.

[197] Cf. G. Braulik, *Die Mittel deuteronomischer Rhetorik* (1978) 58.

[198] Cf. v. 23, where the initial פן parallels "forget" + "covenant" and "make" + "image".

fire". Thereby Yahweh is presented, not only as jealous, but also as merciful. This means that there still is hope for a future for Israel, provided she repents and begins obeying Yahweh's voice.

Secondly, this raises the question for the more general relationship between our passage and the Second commandment. There is a very interesting structural relationship between the two, which can be set up like this:

	Deut 5:8–10 (C)	Deut 4:25–31 (A)
Actor	Future generations	Future generations
Reference	Commandment against images	Commandment against images
Result	Mutually Exclusive alternatives	Chronologically subsequent periods:
	• either Violate the commandment	• first Violate the commandment
	Consequence: Yahweh's punishment, 3–4 generations	*Consequence*: Yahweh's punishment, exile
	• or Keep the commandment	• then Repentance
	Consequence: Yahweh's mercy, thousand generations	*Consequence*: Yahweh's compassion, return

This passage in Deut 4 is often interpreted as reflecting extra-biblical treaty forms; whereas the treaty form presents curse and blessing as alternative possibilities following on disobedience and obedience to the law, this passage, it is argued, rather sees them as successive events connected by repentance and forgiveness.[199] This understanding of the

---

[199]   For a discussion, cf. G. Braulik, *Die Mittel deuteronomischer Rhetorik* (1978) 101–104, and *idem, Deuteronomium 1–16,17* (1986) 39, 44. Of other examples, cf. for example A.D.H. Mayes, "Exposition of

passage presupposes that the interpretation of the Second commandment has come to an end with the third explicit reference to the opening words of the commandment in v. 25. However, as I have argued above, this is not the case. The structural parallelism between this passage and the latter half of the Second commandment is very clear, and one should therefore, I think, interpret the passage with reference to the Second commandment rather than to the treaty forms.

We notice that both the commandment version and our passage relate the Second commandment to the future generations. And we also notice that both categorize the result of this relationship as a double set of consequences, according to how the future generations in practice relate to the commandment. However, the two texts conceptualize the categorizing differently. On the one hand, the Decalogue version categorizes the consequences of the relationship between the commandment and the future generations as mutually exclusive alternatives. The will of Yahweh is clear, there are to be no images. Israel will therefore either break the commandment, and then experience the punishment of Yahweh for three or four generations, or she will keep the commandment, and then experience the mercy of Yahweh for a thousand generations. On the other hand, however, the passage here in Deut 4 categorizes the two possibilities chronologically: they represent successive periods in the history of Israel. Shortly after (the death of Moses, cf. Deut 4:21–22 and 31:29, and) the crossing of the river Jordan, Israel will start breaking the commandment. Eventually, Yahweh will scatter her among the nations (v. 27), and there, in exile, more breaking of the commandment will constitute an important aspect of the punishment (v. 28). But then, in exile, she will repent her sins, turn to Yahweh again, return to obeying his voice, and then she will ultimately meet a merciful God.

Interpretive accent

What is then the interpretive accent of vv. 25–31's allusions to the Second commandment? One thing is that it continues the linking of the previous passages of god and image. More specifically for this particular passage, though, is that it reflects typical Deuteronomistic terminology

---

Deuteronomy 4:25–31", *Irish Biblical Studies* 2 (1980) 79–80, and *idem*, *Deuteronomy* (1979) 156.

related to the exile. When this is combined with structural references to the Second commandment, it creates the impression of a passage that uses the commandment as an hermeneutical key to interpret the exile.

It hardly comes as a surprise that Deut 4 interprets the exile in the light of the Second commandment, as Israel's breaking of the two first commandments constitutes a major reason for the exile, according to Deuteronomistic historiography. Nevertheless, the present passage reflects a somewhat surprising optimism with regard to the future, as there is a development from exilic punishment to post-exilic mercy. A rhetorical means of expressing this development is found in vv. 27–29's triple repetition of the key word שם, "there"; first it is argued that the exile is the context "to where" (שמה) Yahweh will be scattering the people of Israel, then it is said that Israel "there" (שם) in exile will serve gods fashioned by the hands of man, but then, finally, it is also said that Israel "from there" (משם) will seek Yahweh. This optimism with regard to the future comes as a natural consequence of the passage's interpretation of the exile in the light of the Second commandment. The three to four generations of the commandment are usually understood quite literally as referring to the extended family in ancient Israelite society, and the thousand generations are then understood as a contrastive exaggeration.[200] However, when the two options of the commandment are taken to represent chronologically successive periods in the history of Israel, as they are here in Deut 4, the three or four generations of exilic punishment are indeed overshaddowed by the thousand generations of post-exilic mercy. And the passage therefore concludes that Yahweh is a merciful God, who will not destroy Israel and not forget the covenant he made with an oath to the fathers.

---

[200] Cf. for example W.H. Schmidt & al., *Die Zehn Gebote im Rahmen alttestamentlicher Ethik* (1993) 68, and most current commentaries on the Decalogue.

• CHAPTER EIGHT •

FRAME

ANALYSIS OF VV. 1-8 AND 32-40

We have come to an end of the analysis of the core text of Deut 4, vv. 9–31. Still, we have two passages left in Deut 4, the ones that frame this core, vv. 1–8 and 32–40. Let us take a brief look at these passages too.

[1] *And now, O Israel, listen to the decrees and judgements which I teach you to do, so that you may live and enter and take possession of the land which Yahweh, the God of your fathers, gives you.* [2] *You shall not add to the word which I command you, nor take from it, so that you may keep the commandments of Yahweh your God which I command you.* [3] *Your eyes have seen what Yahweh did at Baal Peor, for Yahweh your God destroyed from your midst every man who followed Baal Peor.* [4] *But you who held fast to Yahweh your God are all alive today.* [5] *See, I have taught you decrees and judgements, as Yahweh my God commanded me, to do them in the midst of the land which you are entering to take possession of.* [6] *Keep them and do them, for that will be your wisdom and your understanding in the eyes of the peoples, who, when they hear all these decrees, will say, "Surely, this great nation is a wise and understanding people."* [7] *For what great nation is there that has a god so near to it as is Yahweh our God whenever we call upon him?* [8] *And what great nation is there that has decrees and judgements as just as all this teaching which I set before you this day?*

³² For ask now of the former days that were before you, since the day that God created man upon the earth, from one end of heaven to the other. Has such a great thing as this ever happened, or was something like this ever heard of? ³³ Has any people ever heard the voice of a god speaking out of the midst of the fire, as you have heard, and survived? ³⁴ Or has any god ever attempted to go and take a nation for himself from the midst of another nation, by trials, by signs, and by wonders, and by war, and by a mighty hand, and by an outstretched arm, and by great terrors, as Yahweh your God did for you in Egypt before your eyes? ³⁵ To you this has been shown, so that you might know that Yahweh is God, there is no other besides him. ³⁶ From heaven he let you hear his voice, to instruct you. And on earth he let you see his great fire, and his words you heard out of the midst of the fire. ³⁷ Because he loved your fathers and chose his descendants after him, he brought you out of Egypt with his own presence, by his great power, ³⁸ driving out before you nations greater and mightier than yourselves, to bring you and give to you their land for an inheritance, as it is today. ³⁹ Know therefore today, and lay it to your heart, that Yahweh is God in heaven above and on the earth below, there is no other. ⁴⁰ Keep his decrees and his judgements, which I command you today, that it may go well with you and with your children after you, and that you may prolong your days in the land which Yahweh your God gives you for ever.

I argued in ch. 1 that the two frame passages show signs of a concentric structure around the core text; one example is the thematic, terminological, and structural inclusio of vv. 1–2 and 40, another is the existence of several cases of thematic and structural parallelism between the rest of the two passages.   An outline of these various examples of parallelisms, acknowledging the existence of three sets of concentric circles, would then look like this:

A	B	C	C^I	B^I	A^I
1–2	3–4	5–8	32–34	35–39	40
Law and land	Israel's experience of the judging acts of Yahweh in the past	Israel's incomparability as observing Yahweh's law: 2x rhetorical מִ-questions	Yahweh's incomparability as handling with Israel: 2x rhetorical הַ-questions	Israel's experience of the saving acts of Yahweh in the past	Law and land

Proceeding from this outline, the two framing passages will therefore be analyzed from three perspectives, starting from the core: (1) the inner concentric circle focusing on incomparability, (2) the middle circle focusing on Israel's historical experiences, (3) the outer circle focusing on law and land.

Incomparability: vv. 5–8 and 32–34

The inner concentric circle's focus on incomparability is from a structural perspective characterized by two sets of two rhetorical questions, vv. 7–8 and 33–34. The first set, vv. 7–8, focuses on the incomparability of Israel, and its two מי-questions show a clear parallel structure from the beginning of the verses:

v. 7	כי	מי־גוי גדול	אשר־לו	אלהים קרבים אליו	כיהוה אלהינו
v. 8		ומי גוי גדול	אשר־לו	חקים ומשפטים צדיקם	ככל התורה הזאת

The initial parallelism between the two verses serves to accentuate what is thought to constitute the incomparability of Israel. In spite of her being a "great nation", her greatness is not due to being "the largest of all nations" (cf. Deut 7:7–8), rather to two facts, expressed in two parallel phrases: she has a god in her midst, a god that is identified (-כ) as Yahweh our God (v. 7), and she has decrees and judgements, characterized as just, and identified (-כ) as התורה הזאת, "this teaching" (v. 8).

In the second set of rhetorical questions, vv. 33–34, the focus on Israel is exchanged for a focus on Yahweh and his incomparability. V. 32 invites Israel to ask in time (since creation of man) and space (from one end of the sky to the other) whether such things ever happened or was heard of. This is expressed through two preliminary ה-questions, which prepare for the two following and more substantial, rhetorical ה-questions. These come in vv. 33–34, and here, too, the two questions have a clear and parallel structure from the beginning of the verses:

v. 33	השמע	עם	קול אלהים מדבר	כאשר־שמעת	אתה ויחי
v. 34	או	הנסה	אלהים	לבוא לקחת לו גוי	ככל אשר־עשה	לכם יהוה

In the same way as in the previous set of rhetorical questions, the initial parallelism between these two verses serves to accentuate what is thought to constitute the incomparability, here of Yahweh. It is expressed through two parallel phrases: no other god has ever let any people hear his voice speaking from the midst of a fire, like (-כ) Yahweh let Israel do (v. 33), and no other god ever took a nation for himself, by tests and wonders, like (-כ) Yahweh did with Israel (v. 34).

There is, in other words, a mutual relationship between Israel's and Yahweh's respective ways of being incomparable. Israel's incomparability lies in her relationship to Yahweh, demonstarted by her observance of his decrees and judgments. And likewise, Yahweh's incomparability lies in his relationship to Israel, demonstrated by his speaking to and salvation of his people. The function of this mutual relationship is then to challenge Israel to continue observing Yahweh's decrees and judgements, so that the wisdom reflected in these decrees and judgements can be realized as the wisdom of a "great nation" by the other nations (vv. 5–6).[201]

Historical experience: vv. 3–4 and 35–39

The mutual relationship between Yahweh and Israel, according to vv. 5–8 and 32–34, is then exemplified in two historical cases in the middle concentric circle.

The perspective of the first case, vv. 3–4, is Yahweh's judging acts in the past. The passage refers to an incident said to have happened at Baal Peor, where Yahweh destroyed everyone who followed Baal Peor, whereas those who clung to Yahweh survived. The exact meaning of this brief reference is not clear; however, the terminology that is used—the combination of "followed (הלך אחרי) Baal Peor" and "Yahweh destroyed (שמד, hiph.)"—is enough to indicate that the text refers to some non-yahwistic cultic activity. From a literary perspective, the reference to the Baal Peor incident is related to, and possibly caused by, the literary

---

[201] G. Braulik, "Weisheit, Gottesnähe und Gesetz – Zum Kerygma von Deuteronomium 4,5–8" [1977], G. Braulik, *Studien zur Theologie des Deuteronomiums* (1988) 53–93, suggests to read the double word pair בינה/חכמה and נבון/חכם in v. 6 in the light of the Solomonic wisdom tradition, outlining a new, exilic wisdom, where Yahweh's presence now is seen through Israel's keeping the law.

context's geographical reference to "the ravine opposite Bet Peor", cf. Deut 3:29 and 4:46.[202] But apart from this, one has to search outside Deuteronomy and the Deuteronomistic History for further references. The closest parallels are found in Ps 106, Hos 9 and Num 25,[203] and here the common denominator is a persistent polemic against non-yahwistic religion.[204]

The perspective of the second set of cases, vv. 35–39, is Yahweh's saving acts in the past. It is often argued that when this passage refers to the Horeb theophany (v. 36), the exodus from Egypt (v. 37), and the beginning occupation of the land (v. 38), it just repeats the preceding vv. 33–34.[205] This is, however, not entirely correct. Not only is the material of vv. 33–34 somewhat expanded here to include a more detailed presentation, but the saving acts are also given a more explicit purpose. Rhetorically, this purpose is expressed by an accumulation of the preposition -ל: Yahweh lets Israel hear his voice "to instruct you" (ליסרך), and he brings Israel out of Egypt "to drive out" (להוריש) the other nations, "to bring you" (להביאך) to their land, and "to give [their land] to you" (לתת־לך) for an inheritance.

These two cases of Israel's historical experiences with Yahweh serve to challenge Israel to realize Yahweh's uniqueness. The first case concludes that only those who clung to Yahweh survived, and the second set of cases is framed with an explicit emphasizing of his uniqueness: there is no other, אין עוד, vv. 35 and 39.

---

[202] Cf. J.G. Millar, "Living at the place of decision", J.G. McConville & J.G. Millar, *Time and Place in Deuteronomy* (1994) 41, who, discussing the relationship between Bet Peor and Baal Peor, argues: "It seems likely that this is a deliberate alteration by the Deuteronomist to invest Peor with paradigmatic significance as an archetypal place of apostasy."

[203] A reference in Deut 4 to Num 25 would be yet another sign of Deut 4 being a late text, whose literary horizon is the finalizing of the Pentateuch as a whole and not only that of Deuteronomy; cf. E. Otto, *Das Deuteronomium im Pentateuch und Hexateuch* (2000) *passim*.

[204] For a recent, extensive analysis of the Baal Peor episode in Num 25, emphasizing its main message as a warning against worship of other gods, cf. B.A. Levine, *Numbers 21–36* (2000) 279–303. For a more general analysis of the Baal Peor texts, cf. G.R. Boudreau, "Hosea and the Pentateuchal traditions", M.P. Graham et al. (eds.), *History and Interpretation* (1993) 121–132.

[205] Cf. for example D. Knapp, *Deuteronomium 4* (1987) 111.

Law and land: vv. 1–2 and 40

Finally, the outer concentric circle, vv. 1–2 and 40. Recent scholarship has noticed several examples of a correspondence between vv. 1 and 40, and it has been argued that the two verses to some extent are parallel both from thematic and terminological perspectives. The similarities between the two have led some scholars, for example G. Braulik and M. Weinfeld,[206] to acknowledge an inclusio that frames and binds vv. 1–40 together as one unit, and that reflects a single authorship, whereas others, not least D. Knapp,[207] argue that there are still important differences between the two, and that these reflect different authors. Let us take a closer look at the structure and terminology of the two verses.

[...] מלמד אנכי אשר ואל־המשפטים אל־החקים שמע [...]	v. 1a
[...] מצוך אנכי אשר ואת־מצותיו את־חקיו ושמרת	v. 40a
נתן לכם [...] אשר יהוה את־הארץ [...] תחיו למען	v. 1b
[...] נתן לך [...] אשר יהוה על־האדמה ימים תאריך ולמען	v. 40b

Two things are clear from this survey. First, the two verses are indeed parallel, not only from thematic and terminological perspectives, but also structurally. As such it should be demonstrated that they may serve as an inclusio of Deut 4:1–40. Secondly, there are also certain differences between the two, but it is difficult to see that these have important, interpretive significance. Some of the differences can easily be explained as reflecting a need even within Deuteronomistic literature for some terminological variation; see, for example, v. 1b's ארץ versus v. 40b's אדמה. Others may, however, reflect some interpretive difference. One example is v. 1a's word pair חקים/משפטים versus v. 40a's word pair חקים/מצות;[208] here, the latter's introduction of מצות instead of משפטים serves to link v. 2 to the inclusio, a verse which else would fall outside

---

[206]   Cf. G. Braulik, *Die Mittel deuteronomischer Rhetorik* (1978) 64, 86–87; M. Weinfeld, *Deuteronomy 1–11* (1991) 199.

[207]   Cf. D. Knapp, *Deuteronomium 4* (1987) 110.

[208]   To the different terms for "law", cf. G. Braulik, "Die Ausdrücke für 'Gesetz' im Buch Deuteronomium", *Biblica* 51 (1970) 39–66.

the concentric structure.[209] Another example is a possible sharpening from v. 1a's verb pair שָׁמַע and לָמַד to v. 40a's parallel verb pair שָׁמַר and צוה.

Taken as a whole, the outer concentric circle challenges Israel, in a typical Deuteronomistic form, to focus on Yahweh's decrees, judgements and commandments, as they are given by Moses, and with the purpose (2x לְמַעַן) of preparing Israel for the life in the promised land.

---

[209] Cf. G. Braulik, *Die Mittel deuteronomischer Rhetorik* (1978) 87. D. Knapp, *Deuteronomium 4* (1987) 110, is of the opposite meaning, arguing that "Daß dabei eine andere Hand am Werke ist, wird an den unterschiedlichen bezeichnungen für das Gesetz ein weiteres Mal sichtbar".

• CHAPTER NINE •

CONCLUSION

What are then the interpretive accents of Deut 4's interpretation of the Second commandment? In a most influential article written half a century ago, W. Zimmerli touches on this topic, and he argues:

> Die Vermutung legt sich sehr nahe, daß Dt. 4,9ff. als Auslegung des dekalogischen Bildverbotes entstanden ist. Es wäre dabei sicher nicht richtig, Dt. 4 als authentische Interpretation des Bildverbotes zu bezeichnen und zu behaupten, daß die recht eigenwilligen Gedanken von Dt. 4 schon im Bewußtsein dessen, der das zweite Gebot verfaßte […] gelegen hätten.[210]

I agree. Deut 4 is of course no "authentic interpretation", whatever that could be, of the Second commandment. Rather, Deut 4 is an attempt by some unknown interpreter at relating the commandment to this particular interpreter's contextual concerns and theological universe, and as such its interpretive accents, which have been analyzed successively in the previous chapters, obviously reflect what Zimmerli calls this interpreter's "eigenwilligen Gedanken". Let me here, in conclusion, restrict myself to make a few remarks concerning two of these interpretive accents, one is the paraenetic setting of the interpretation, the other is its concept of images.

---

[210] W. Zimmerli, "Das zweite Gebot", *Gottes Offenbarung* ([1950] 1963) 247.

First, and hardly surprising, as it is quite typical to Deuteronomy, we notice that Deut 4's paraenesis on the Second commandment is legitimized by repeated references to Israel's historical experiences with Yahweh. The two first passages refer to the Horeb theophany, letting the form of the theophany—verbal, rather than visual—be used as a theological rationale for the prohibition against images (vv. 9–14, 15). This initial historification is then followed up by the subsequent passages, where the paraenesis on the Second commandment is related to Israel's experience of being saved from Egypt (vv. 19–20), her rebellion against Yahweh in the desert, her crossing of the river Jordan, her occupation of the promised land (vv. 21–24), and finally to the exile and its hope for a future (vv. 25–31). The same tendency of relating the paraenesis to history is also reflected in the frame passages, which refer to Israel's judging (vv. 3–4) and saving (vv. 35–39) experiences with Yahweh.

The final references of this historical exposé, those related to the exile, are of particular importance, as they relate the Second commandment explicitly to the exilic or early post-exilic context of Deut 4's first readers. On the one hand, the references to the exile, especially in vv. 25–31, demonstrate that the hope for the future is not unconditioned; it provides that Israel repents her sins and turns to Yahweh. As M. Weinfeld has demonstrated, this passage is part of a broad material of texts on repentance, from various parts of the Deuteronomistic movement, for example 1 Kings 8, Hos 5–6, and Jer 29.[211] However, on the other hand, whereas most examples within this material have a quite strong hortatory emphasis, the examples we meet here in vv. 25–29 are of a more proclamative character.[212] Compared for example to Hos 5:5–6:1 and its cohortative "let us return (ונשובה) to Yahweh" (6:1), our passage has an indicative "you will return (ושבת) to Yahweh" (v. 30). This indicative expresses a clear and confident hope for the future; some day Israel will indeed seek Yahweh, with her whole heart and whole soul, and she will then live in the land forever. What we encounter in the final passage of the core text of Deut 4 is therefore not what D. Knapp and many other interpreters call an invitation to conversion,[213] but rather what H.W. Wolff many years ago, in his epoch-

---

[211]   Cf. M. Weinfeld, *Deuteronomy 1–11* (1991) 217–221.

[212]   Cf. A. Graupner, "שוב", *Theologisches Wörterbuch zum Alten Testament* 7 (1993) 1155.

[213]   Cf. D. Knapp, *Deuteronomium 4* (1987) 91.

making study on the kerygma of the Deuteronomistic History, called *Verheißungsgut*.[214] Even though Deut 4's imagination of Israel's hope for the future provides that she repents her sins and turns to Yahweh, there is a clear confidence that so will eventually be the case, a confidence which points in the direction of other late exilic texts, not least Second Isaiah's proclamation of salvation.

Secondly, and more surprising, as it is not that typical to Deuteronomy, is Deut 4's profiled concept of images. One example is vv. 16b–18's portrayal of the image in a language that relates it to the concept of the creation of humankind. The interpretation of the Second commandment which here is reflected seems to understand the making of images in the likeness of humankind and other creatures as contrary to Israel's belief in Yahweh as creator of humankind and all other creatures; humankind even being created in the image of God. Deut 4 is here quite close to some other significant theological concepts of the exile; one example is the Priestly creation theology, another is Second Isaiah's religious polemics.[215] The same can also be said about another example of Deut 4's profiled concept of the image, the gradual development with regard to focus throughout the core text, from images of Yahweh (v. 15), via images (vv. 16–18) and other gods (vv. 19–20), to other gods,

---

[214] Cf. H.W. Wolff, "Das Kerygma des deuteronomistischen Geschichtswerk", *ZAW* 73 (1961) 171–186, where he observes that "Vor allem die zweite Hand des dtr. Kreises, die wir wahrscheinlich in Dtn 4:29–31 und 30:1–10 zu sehen haben, zeigt deutlich daß DtrG die Umkehr weniger als menschliche Tat denn vielmehr als eine Frucht des Gerichts ansieht, die als solche von Jahwe verheißen is, nachdem das Volk vor dem Gericht dem prophetischen Mahnruf zur Umkehr keinen Gehorsam leistete", p. 184.

[215] Several corresponding examples may be found in Second Isaiah's polemics against idol-fabrication. One example is Isa 44:13, where an idol is presented as תבנית איש ("the likeness of a man", cf. the parallel in Deut 4:16, תבנית זכר או נקבה, "the likeness of male or female"), and where the literary context, Isa 44:9–20, ironically portrays the idol-fabricator as having taken the role of Yahweh: he makes an idol in the likeness of himself. Another example is a rhetorical question found in Isa 40:18.25 and 46:5, ironically challenging the audience to point out a דמות for God ("likeness", cf. Gen 1:26's כדמותנו, "after our likeness"), where, again, the literary context, Isa 40:19–20 and 46:6–7, responds with an ironical portrayal of the idol-fabricator that have taken the role of Yahweh and made a god in the likeness of man. For a closer analysis, cf. K. Holter, *Second Isaiah's Idol-fabrication Passages* (1995) 79–89, 163–167.

explicitly identified as images (v. 28). As I have pointed out several times in the previous chapters, the interpretation of the Second commandment which is expressed here seems to draw it in the direction of the First commandment's prohibition against other gods than Yahweh. I would like to emphasize, though, that this does not mean that the Second commandment is subordinated the First, so that the "image" warned against here simply refers to images of the "other gods" of the First commandment. What is outlined in Deut 4 is rather that the two commandments complement each other. In their Decalogue versions, the emphasis of the First commandment is not the "other gods", but Yahweh's uniqueness, and, likewise, the emphasis of the Second commandment is not the "image", but how to secure Yahweh's uniqueness. Here in Deut 4 a corresponding emphasis on the uniqueness of Yahweh is expressed in the inner concentric frame passages. And I would tend to argue that Deut 4's interpretation of the Second commandment intends to prevent Yahweh from being understood like the other gods, who are known through their images.[216]

Interpretation of Old Testament texts is never static, never mere repetition. Rather, it is an ongoing process, where the contextual concerns and theological universe of the interpreter interact with the source text, finding new interpretive potentials in this text. So is also the case with Deut 4's interpretation of the Second commandment. The commandment is related to the theological universe and contextual needs of its unknown exilic or early post-exilic interpreter, and the result is a text that is an inspiration to all subsequent interpreters of the Second commandment.

---

[216]   Here, too, Second Isaiah's polemics against idol-fabrication provides clear parallels. One example is the identification of god and idol (cf. for example 44:15.17). Another is the series of rhetorical מי-questions which introduce the four idol-fabrication passages (cf. 40:18/19–20, 41:4/6–7, 44:7/9–20, 46:5/6–7), a series that has the rhetorical function of accentuating Yahweh's incomparability. For a closer analysis, cf. K. Holter, *Second Isaiah's Idol-fabrication Passages* (1995) 203–206.

BIBLIOGRAPHY

Aichele, G. & Philips, G.A. (eds.), *Intertextuality and the Bible*. Atlanta, 1995 (*Semeia* 69–70).

Andersen, F.I. & Forbes, A.D., *The Vocabulary of the Old Testament*. Rome, 1992.

Begg, C.T., "The literary criticism of Deut 4,1–40: Contributions to a continuing discussion", *Ephemerides Theologicae Lovanienses* 56 (1980) 10–55.

Ben-Porrat, Z., "The poetics of literary allusion", *PTL: A Journal for Descriptive Poetics and Theory of Literature* 1 (1976) 105–128.

Berlejung, A., *Die Theologie der Bilder: Herstellung und Einweihung von Kultbildern in Mesopotamien und in die alttestamentliche Bilderpolemik*. Freiburg & Göttingen, 1998 (Orbis Biblicus et Orientalis; 162).

Boudreau, G.R., "Hosea and the Pentateuchal traditions", M.P. Graham & al. (eds.), *History and Interpretation: Essays in Honour of John H. Hayes*. Sheffield (1993) 121–132 (Journal for the Study of the Old Testament Supplement Series; 173).

Braulik, G., "Die Ausdrücke für 'Gesetz' im Buch Deuteronomiums", *Biblica* 51 (1970) 39–66.

———, *Die Mittel deuteronomischer Rhetorik: Erhoben aus Deuteronomium 4,1–40*. Rome, 1978 (Analecta Biblica; 68).

———, "Literarkritik und archäologische Stratigraphie. Zu S. Mittmanns Analyse von Deuteronomium 4,1–40", *Biblica* 59 (1978) 351–383.

———, *Deuteronomium 1–16,17*. Würzburg 1986 (Neue Echter Bibel: Kommentar zum Alten Testament).

————, *Deuteronomium 16,18–34,12*. Würzburg 1992 (Neue Echter Bibel: Kommentar zum Alten Testament).

————, "Weisheit, Gottesnähe und Gesetz: Zum Kerygma von Deuteronomium 4,5–8" [1977], G. Braulik, *Studien zur Theologie des Deuteronomiums*. Stuttgart (1988) 53–93.

————, "Literarkritik und die einrahmung von Gemälden: Zur literarkritischen und redaktionsgeschichtlichen Analyse von Dtn 4,1–6,3 und 29,1–30,10 durch D. Knapp", *Revue Biblique* 96 (1989) 266–286.

Brown, F. & al., *The New Brown-Driver-Briggs-Gesenius Hebrew and English Lexicon*. Peabody, 1979.

Christensen, D.L., "Prose and poetry in the Bible: The narrative poetics of Deuteronomy 1,9–18", *Zeitschrift für die alttestamentliche Wissenschaft* 97 (1985) 179–189.

————, "Form and structure in Deuteronomy 1–11", N. Lohfink (ed.), *Das Deuteronomium: Entstehung, Gestalt und Botschaft*. Leuven (1985) 135–144 (Bibliotheca Ephmeridum Theologicarum Lovaniensium; 68).

————, *Deuteronomy 1–11*. Dallas, 1991 (Word Biblical Commentary; 6a).

Dietrich, M. & Loretz, O., *'Jahwe und seine Aschera': Anthropomorphes Kultbild im Mesopotamien, Ugarit und Israel. Das biblische Bilderverbot*. Münster, 1992 (Ugaritisch-Biblische Literatur; 9).

Dillmann, A., *Die Bücher Numeri, Deuteronomium und Josua*. Leipzig 1886 (Kurzgefasstes exegetisches Handbuch zum Alten Testament).

Dohmen, C., "פסל—פסיל: Zwei Nominalbildungen von פסל?", *Biblische Notizen* 16 (1981) 11–12.

————, "Heißt סמל 'Bild, Statue'?", *Zeitschrift für die alttestamentliche Wissenschaft* 96 (1984) 263–266.

————, *Das Bilderverbot: Seine Entstehung und seine Entwicklung im Alten Testament*. Frankfurt am Main, 1987² (Bonner Biblische Beiträge; 62).

————, "פסל", *Theologisches Wörterbuch zum Alten Testament* 6 (1989) 688–697.

Driver, S.R., *A Critical and Exegetical Commentary on Deuteronomy*. Edinburgh [1895] 1978³ (International Critical Commentary).

Eissfeldt, O., *Hexateuch-Synopse: Die Erzählung der 5 Bücher Mose und des Buches Josua mit dem Anfange des Richterbuches in ihre 4 Quellen zerlegt [...]*. Leipzig, 1922.

Eslinger, L., "Inner-biblical exegesis and inner-biblical allusion: The question of category", *Vetus Testamentum* 42 (1992) 47–58.

Evans, C.A. & Talmon, S. (eds.), *The Quest for Context and Meaning: Studies in Biblical Intertextuality in Honor of James A. Sanders*. Leiden, 1997 (Biblical Interpretation Series; 28).

Fewell, D.N. (ed.), *Reading between Texts: Intertextuality and the Hebrew Bible.* Louisville, 1992 (Literary Currents in Biblical Interpretation).

Fishbane, M., "Varia Deuteronomica", *Zeitschrift für die alttestamentliche Wissenschaft* 84 (1972) 349–352

——, "Numbers 5:11–31: A study of law and scribal practice in Israel and the Ancient Near East", *Hebrew Union College Annual* 45 (1974) 25–43.

——, "The Qumran Pesher and traits of ancient hermeneutics", *Proceedings of the Sixth World Congress of Jewish Studies* 1 (1977) 97–114.

——, "Torah and tradition", D.A. Knight (ed.), *Tradition and Theology in the Old Testament.* London (1977) 275–300.

——, "On colophons, textual criticism and legal analogies", *Catholic Biblical Quarterly* 42 (1980) 438–449.

——, "Revelation and tradition: Aspects of inner-biblical exegesis", *Journal of Biblical Literature* 99 (1980) 343–361.

——, *Biblical Interpretation in Ancient Israel.* Oxford, 1985.

——, *The Garnments of Torah: Essays in Biblical Hermeneutics.* Bloomington, 1989 (Indiana Studies in Biblical Literature).

——, "Inner-biblical exegesis", M. Sæbø (ed.), *Hebrew Bible / Old Testament: The History of its Interpretation: From the Beginnings to the Middle Ages (until 1300). I/1.* Göttingen (1996) 33–48.

——, "'Orally write therefore aurally right': An essay on Midrash", C.A. Evans & S. Talmon (eds.), *The Quest for Context and Meaning: Studies in Biblical Intertextuality in Honor of James A. Sanders.* Leiden (1997) 531–546 (Biblical Interpretation Series; 28).

——, "The Hebrew Bible and exegetical tradition", J.C. de Moor (ed.), *Intertextuality in Ugarit and Israel: Papers read at the Tenth Joint Meeting of the Society for Old Testament Study and Het Oudtestamentisch Werkgezelschap in Nederland en Belgie Held at Oxford, 1997.* Leiden (1998) 15–30 (Oudtestamentische Studiën; 40).

——, "Types of biblical intertextuality", A. Lemaire & M. Sæbø (eds.), *Congress Volume Oslo 1998.* Leiden (2000) 39–44 (Supplements to Vetus Testamentum; 80).

Floss, J.P., *Jahwe dienen - Göttern dienen. Terminologische, literarische und semantische Untersuchung einer theologische Aussage zum Gottesverhältnis im Alten Testament.* Köln, 1975 (Bonner Biblische Beiträge; 45).

Frevel, C., "Die Elimination der Göttin aus dem Weltbild des Chronisten", *Zeitschrift für die alttestamentliche Wissenschaft* 103 (1991) 263–271.

García-Lopez, F., "נגד", *Theologisches Wörterbuch zum Alten Testament* 5 (1986) 188–201.

————, "שָׁמַר", *Theologisches Wörterbuch zum Alten Testament* 8 (1995) 280–306.

Geller, S.A., "Fiery wisdom", S.A. Geller, *Sacred Enigmas: Literary Religion in the Hebrew Bible*. London & New York (1996) 30–61.

Gesenius, W., *Hebräisches und aramäisches Handwörterbuch über Das Alte Testament*. Berlin, 1962[17].

Graupner, A., "Zum Verhältnis der beiden Dekalogfassungen Ex 20 und Dtn 5: Ein Gespräch mit Frank-Lothar Hossfeld", *Zeitschrift für die alttestamentliche Wissenschaft* 99 (1987) 308–329.

————, "שׁוב", *Theologisches Wörterbuch zum Alten Testament* 7 (1993) 1118–1176.

Greenberg, M., *Ezekiel 1–20*. New York 1986 (The Anchor Bible; 22A).

Herrmann, S., "[Rec. of] G. Braulik, *Die Mittel Deuteronomischer Rhetoric*", *Theologische Revue* 77 (1981) 10–12.

Holter, K., *Second Isaiah's Idol-fabrication Passages*. Frankfurt am Main, 1995 (Beiträge zur biblischen Exegese und Theologie; 28).

————, "Literary critical studies of Deut 4: Some criteriological remarks", *Biblische Notizen* 81 (1996) 91–103.

Hossfeld, F.-L., *Der Dekalog: Seine späte Fassungen, die originale Komposition und seine Vorstufen*. Freiburg & Göttingen, 1982 (Orbis Biblicus et Orientalis; 45).

————, "Du sollst dir kein Bild machen! Die Funktion des alttestamentlichen Bilderverbots", *Trierer theologische Zeitschrift* 98 (1989) 81–94.

————, "Zum synoptischen Vergleich der Dekalogfassungen: Eine Fortführung des begonnenen Gesprächs", F.-L. Hossfeld (ed.), *Vom Sinai zum Horeb: Stationen alttestamentlicher Glaubensgeschichte*. Würzburg (1989) 73–117.

Joüon, P. & Muraoka, T., *A Grammar of Biblical Hebrew*. Rome, 1991 (Subsidia Biblica 14/I & 14/II).

Keel, O. & Uehlinger, C., *Göttinnen, Götter und Gottessymbole: Neue Erkenntnisse zur Religionsgeschichte Kanaans und Israels aufgrund bislang unerschlossener ikonographischer Quellen*. Freiburg, 1992.

Knapp, D., *Deuteronomium 4. Literarische Analyse und theologische Interpretation*. Göttingen, 1987 (Göttinger Theologische Arbeiten; 35).

Kraus, H.-J., *Psalmen 60–150*. Neukirchen-Vluyn, 1978[5] (Biblischer Kommentar Altes Testament; XV/2).

Kuenen, A., *An Historico-Critical Inquiry into the Origin and Composition of the Hexateuch*. London, 1886 [Originally publ. as a part of the three vols. series *Historisch-Kritisch Onderzoek naar het ontstaan en de verzameling van de Boecken des Ouden Verbonds.* Leiden 1861–1865; this translation follows the 2. ed. of the Hexateuch, Leiden, 1885].

Labuschagne, C.J., *Deuteronomium IA.* Nijkerk, 1987 (De Prediking van het Oude Testament).

———, *Deuteronomium IB.* Nijkerk, 1987 (De Prediking van het Oude Testament).

Lemaire, A. & Sæbø, M. (eds.), *Congress Volume Oslo 1998.* Leiden, 2000 (Supplements to Vetus Testamentum; 80).

Levenson, J.D., "Who inserted the Book of the Torah?", *Harvard Theological Review* 68 (1975) 203–233.

Levine, B.A., *Numbers 21–36.* New York, 2000 (The Anchor Bible; 4A).

Levinson, B.M., *Deuteronomy and the Hermeneutics of Legal Innovation.* New York, 1997.

Loersch, S., *Das Deuteronomium und seine Deutungen: Ein forschungsgeschichtlicher Überblick.* Stuttgart 1967 (Stuttgarter Bibelstudien; 22).

Lohfink, N., *Das Hauptgebot: Eine Untersuchung literarischer Einleitungsfragen zu Dtn 5–11.* Rome, 1963 (Analecta Biblica; 20).

———, "Auslegung deuteronomischer Texte. IV. Verkündigung des Hauptgebots in der jüngsten Schicht des Deuteronomium (Dt 4,1–40)", *Bibel und Leben* 5 (1964) 247–256; republ. in an expanded version as "Verkündigung des Hauptgebots in der jüngsten Schicht des Deuteronomiums (Dt 4:1–40)" [1965], N. Lohfink, *Studien zum Deuteronomium und zur deuteronomistischen Literatur. I.* Stuttgart (1990) 167–191 (Stuttgarter Biblische Aufsatzbände; 8).

——— (ed.), *Das Deuteronomium: Entstehung, Gestalt und Botschaft.* Leuven, 1985 (Bibliotheca Ephemeridum Theologicarum Lovaniensium; 68).

Lutzky, H.C., "On 'the image of jealousy' (Ezekiel viii 3,5)", *Vetus Testamentum* 46 (1996) 121–125.

Mayes, A.D.H., *Deuteronomy.* Grand Rapids & London, 1979 (The New Century Bible Commentary).

———, "Exposition of Deuteronomy 4:25–31", *Irish Biblical Studies* 2 (1980) 67–83.

———, "Deuteronomy 4 and the literary criticism of Deuteronomy", *Journal of Biblical Literature* 100 (1981) 23–51.

McConville, J.G., *Law and Theology in Deuteronomy.* Sheffield, 1984 (Journal for the Study of the Old Testament Supplement Series; 33).

Mendenhall, G.E., *Law and Covenant in Israel and the Ancient Near East.* Pittsburg, 1955.

Mettinger, T.N.D., *No Graven Image? Israelite Aniconism in its Ancient Near Eastern Context*. Stockholm, 1995 (Coniectanea Biblica: Old Testament Series; 42).

———, "Israelite aniconism: developments and origins", K. Van der Toorn (ed.), *The Image and the Book: Iconic Cults, Aniconism and the Rise of Book Religion in Israel and in the Ancient Near East*. Leuven (1997) 173–204 (Contributions to Biblical Exegesis and Theology; 21).

Millar, J.G., "Living at the place of decision: Time and place in the framework of Deuteronomy", J.G. McConville & J.G. Millar, *Time and Place in Deuteronomy*. Sheffield (1994) 31–88 (Journal for the Study of the Old Testament Supplement Series; 179).

Mittmann, S., *Deuteronomium 1,1–6,3 literarkritisch und traditionsgeschichtlich untersucht*. Berlin, 1975 (Beihefte zur Zeitschrift für die alttestamentliche Wissenschaft; 139).

Moor, J.C. de (ed.), *Intertextuality in Ugarit and Israel: Papers read at the Tenth Joint Meeting of the Society for Old Testament Study and Het Oudtestamentisch Werkgezelschap in Nederland en Belgie Held at Oxford, 1997*. Leiden, 1998 (Oudtestamentische Studiën; 40).

Nielsen, E., *Deuteronomium*. Tübingen, 1995 (Handbuch zum Alten Testament; I/6).

Nielsen, K., "Intertextuality and Hebrew Bible", A. Lemaire & M. Sæbø (eds.), *Congress Volume Oslo 1998*. Leiden (2000) 17–31 (Supplements to Vetus Testamentum; 80).

Noth, M., *Überlieferungsgeschichtliche Studien. Erster Teil. Die sammelenden und bearbeitenden Geschichtswerke im Alten Testament*. Darmstadt, [1943] 1963.

O'Brien, M.A., "The Book of Deuteronomy", *Currents in Research: Biblical Studies* 3 (1995) 95–128.

O'Connell, R.H., "Deuteronomy viii 1–20: Assymetrical concentricity and the rhetoric of providence", *Vetus Testamentum* 40 (1990) 437–452.

Otto, E., "Deuteronomium 4: Die Pentateuchredaktion im Deuteronomiumsrahmen", T. Veijola (ed.), *Das Deuteronomium und seine Querbeziehungen*. Göttingen (1996) 196–222 (Schriften der Finnischen Exegetischen Gesellschaft; 62).

———, *Das Deuteronomium im Pentateuch und Hexateuch: Studien zur Literaturgeschichte von Pentateuch und Hexateuch im Lichte des Deuteronomiumrahmens*. Tübingen, 2000 (Forschungen zum Alten Testament; 30).

Plett, H.F., "Intertextualities", H.F. Plett (ed.), *Intertextuality*. Berlin, 1991 (Research in Text Theory; 15).

Preuss, H.D., *Verspottung fremder Religionen im Alten Testament.* Stuttgart, 1971 (Beiträge zur Wissenschaft vom Alten und Neuen Testament; 92).

————, *Deuteronomium.* Darmstadt, 1982 (Erträge der Forschung; 164).

Rad, G. von, *Das fünfte Buch Mose.* Göttingen 1964 (Das Alte Testament Deutsch; 8).

Reuter, E., "קנא", *Theologisches Wörterbuch zum Alten Testament* 7 (1993) 51–62.

Reventlow, H. Graf, *Gebot und Predigt im Dekalog.* Gütersloh, 1962.

Ringgren, H., "כל", *Theologisches Wörterbuch zum Alten Testament* 4 (1984) 145–153.

Rofé, A., "The monotheistic argumentation in Deuteronomy iv 32–40: Contents, composition and text", *Vetus Testamentum* 35 (1985) 434–445.

Roth, W., (ed.), "Interpretation as scripture matrix: A panel on Fishbane's thesis", *Biblical Research* 35 (1990) 36–57.

Sauer, G., "כל", *Theologisches Handwörterbuch zum Alten Testament* 1 (1984) 828–830.

Schmidt, B.B., "The aniconic tradition: On reading images and viewing texts", D.V. Edelman (ed.), *The Triumph of Elohim: From Yahwisms to Judaisms.* Kampen (1995) 75–105 (Contributions to Biblical Exegesis and Theology; 13).

Schmidt, W.H., "דבר", *Theologisches Wörterbuch zum Alten Testament* 2 (1977) 89–133.

Schmidt, W.H. & al., *Die Zehn Gebote im Rahmen Alttestamentlicher Ethik.* Darmstadt, 1993 (Erträge der Forschung; 281).

Schreiner, J., "ילד", *Theologisches Wörterbuch zum Alten Testament* 3 (1982) 633–639.

Schroer, S., *In Israel gab es Bilder: Nachrichten von darstellender Kunst im Alten Testament.* Freiburg & Göttingen, 1987 (Orbis Biblicus et Orientalis; 74).

Smend, R., *Die Entstehung des Alten Testaments.* Stuttgart, 1981² (Theologische Wissenschaft; 1).

Sommer, B.D., "Exegesis, allusion and intertextuality in the Hebrew Bible: A response to Lyle Eslinger", *Vetus Testamentum* 56 (1996) 479–489.

————, *A Prophet Reads Scripture: Allusion in Isaiah 40-66.* Stanford, 1998 (Contraversions: Jews and other Differences).

Staerk, W., *Das Deuteronomium: Sein Inhalt und seine literarische Form.* Leipzig, 1894.

Steuernagel, C., *Der Rahmen des Deuteronomiums: Literarcritische Untersuchung über seine Zusammensetzung und Entstehung.* Berlin, 1894.

Stordalen, T., *Echoes of Eden: Genesis 2–3 and Symbolism of the Eden Garden in Biblical Hebrew Literature*. Leuven, 2000 (Contributions to Biblical Exegesis and Theology; 25).

Tull, P., "Intertextuality and the Hebrew Scriptures", *Currents in Research: Biblical Studies* 8 (2000) 59–90.

Veijola, T., "Bundestheologische Redaktion im Deuteronomium", T. Veijola (ed.), *Das Deuteronomium und seine Querbeziehungen*. Göttingen (1996) 252–275 (Schriften der Finnischen Exegetischen Gesellschaft; 62).

Vieweger, D., "'... und führte euch heraus aus dem Eisenschmelzoven, aud Ägypten, ...'", P. Mommer & al. (eds.), *Gottes Recht als Lebensraum: Festschrift für Hans Jochen Boecker*. Neukirchen-Vluyn (1993) 265–276.

Wagner, S., "בנה", *Theologisches Wörterbuch zum Alten Testament* 1 (1973) 689–706.

Waschke, E.-J., "תמונה", *Theologisches Wörterbuch zum Alten Testament* 8 (1995) 677–680.

Watson, W.G.E., *Classical Hebrew Poetry: A Guide to its Techniques*. Sheffield 1984 (Journal for the Study of the Old Testament Supplement Series; 26).

Weinfeld, M., *Deuteronomy and the Deuteronomic School*. Oxford, 1972.

———, *Deuteronomy 1–11: A New Translation with Introduction and Commentary*. New York, 1991 (The Anchor Bible; 5).

Westermann, C., *Genesis 1–11*. Neukirchen-Vluyn, 1974 (Biblischer Kommentar Altes Testament; I/1).

Wette, W.M.L. de, *Dissertatio critico-exegetica qua Deuteronomium a prioribus Pentateuchi libris diversum, alius cuiusdam recentioris auctoris opus esse monstratur*. Jena, 1805.

Wilson, I., *Out of the Midst of the Fire: Divine Presence in Deuteronomy*. Atlanta, 1995 (Society of Biblical Literature Dissertation Series; 151).

Wolff, H.W., "Das Kerygma des deuteronomistischen Geschichtswerk", *Zeitschrift für die alttestamentliche Wissenschaft* 73 (1961) 171–186.

Zimmerli, W., "Das zweite Gebot", *Gottes Offenbarung. Gesammelte Aufsätze zum Alten Testament*. München (1963) 234–248 (Theologische Bücherei; 19). [Originally publ. in W. Baumgartner & al. (eds.), *Festschrift Alfred Bertholet zum 80. Geburtstag*. Tübingen (1950) 550–563].

———, *Ezechiel 1–24*. Neukirchen-Vluyn, 1969 (Biblischer Kommentar Altes Testament; XIII/1).

INDEX OF AUTHORS

Hossfeld, F.-L.: 66, 73, 74, 75, 76, 77, 78, 97

Joüon, P.: 40

Keel, O.: 3
Knapp, D.: 3, 7, 8, 11, 12, 30, 31, 32, 38, 39, 44, 48, 52, 56, 57, 58, 61, 62, 66, 77, 80, 81, 87, 105, 106, 107, 110
Kraus, H.-J.: 65
Kuenen, A.: 55

Labuschagne, C.J.: 9, 11, 61, 63, 74
Lemaire, A.: 14
Levenson, J.D.: 8
Levine, B.A.: 105
Levinson, B.M.: 19
Loersch, S.: 6
Lohfink, N.: 7, 9, 50, 51
Loretz, O.: 64
Lutzky, H.C.: 45

Mayes, A.D.H.: 8, 11, 51, 61, 74, 98, 99
McConville, J.G.:
Mendenhall, G.E.: 7
Mettinger, T.N.D.: 3
Millar, J.G.: 10, 105
Mittmann, S.: 8, 11
Moor, J.C. de: 14
Muraoka, T.: 40

Nielsen, E.: 8, 11, 65, 66, 81
Nielsen, K.: 14

Noth, M.: 30, 62, 63

O'Brien, M.A.: 6
O'Connell, R.H.: 50, 51
Otto, E.: 8, 61, 67, 91, 105

Philips, G.A.: 14
Plett, H.F.: 18
Preuss, H.D.: 6, 80

Rad, G. von: 30, 31, 74
Reuter, E.: 90
Reventlow, H. Graf: 74
Ringgren, H.: 41
Rofé, A.: 63
Roth, W.: 17

Sauer, G.: 41
Sæbø, M.: 14
Schmidt, B.B.: 3, 77
Schmidt, W.H.: 24, 76, 100
Schreiner, J.: 63
Schroer, S.: 3
Smend, R.: 57
Sommer, B.D.: 14, 17, 18
Staerk, W.: 7, 55
Steuernagel, C.: 7
Stordalen, T.: 18

Talmon, S.: 14
Tull, P.: 14

Uehlinger, C.: 3

INDEX OF SUBJECTS

INDEX OF BIBLICAL REFERENCES

Studies in Biblical Literature

This series invites manuscripts from scholars in any area of biblical literature. Both established and innovative methodologies, covering general and particular areas in biblical study, are welcome. The series seeks to make available studies that will make a significant contribution to the ongoing biblical discourse. Scholars who have interests in gender and sociocultural hermeneutics are particularly encouraged to consider this series.

For further information about the series and for the submission of manuscripts, contact:

Hemchand Gossai
Department of Religion
Muhlenberg College
2400 Chew Street
Allentown, PA 18104-5586

To order other books in this series, please contact our Customer Service Department:

(800) 770-LANG (within the U.S.)
(212) 647-7706 (outside the U.S.)
(212) 647-7707 FAX

or browse online by series at:

WWW.PETERLANGUSA.COM